The Difficult Second Book

This is the book Chris's publishers
have been waiting for.

JIMMY CARR

CHRIS MOYLES

The Difficult Second Book

EBURY
PRESS

1 3 5 7 9 10 8 6 4 2

Published in 2007 by Ebury Press, an imprint of Ebury Publishing
A Random House Group Company

The Random House Group Limited Reg. No. 954009

Addresses for companies within the Random House Group can be found at
www.randomhouse.co.uk

A CIP catalogue record for this book is available from the British Library

The Random House Group Limited supports The Forest Stewardship Council
(FSC), the leading international forest certification organisation. All our titles that
are printed on Greenpeace approved FSC certified paper carry the FSC logo. Our
paper procurement policy can be found at www.rbooks.co.uk/environment

Mixed Sources
Product group from well-managed
forests and other controlled sources
www.fsc.org Cert no. TT-COC-2139
© 1996 Forest Stewardship Council
FSC

Printed and bound in Great Britain by Clays Ltd, St Ives PLC

HB ISBN 9780091922429
PB ISBN 9780091922436

To buy books by your favourite authors and register for offers visit
www.rbooks.co.uk

Another book? Fuck me! What desperate idiots who don't know any better are going to fork out for another book by Chris Moyles?

NOEL GALLAGHER

Acknowledgements

I'd like to thank everybody who helped with the writing of this book, with special thanks to Miranda my tireless editor, Mari my copy-editor and of course our book lawyer Roger Field.

This book is dedicated to anybody who has laughed out loud during our morning radio show. Thank you.

I think he might be gay, he

definitely fancies me.

DAVID WALLIAMS

CONTENTS

WELCOME,

READER,
TO THE FIRST
PAGE OF TEXT

Hello, and thanks for buying this book. If you haven't bought it and have merely borrowed it or, worse still, stolen a copy, then I think you should know that my charity will now suffer as a result of your tightness. To those of you who have genuinely bought this book, then, from everybody at 'The Chris Moyles Portuguese Villa Fund', may I thank you so much.

So what is *The Difficult Second Book* all about?

Well, let me be honest, and there will be A LOT of honesty throughout this book, the following pages contain humorous and interesting stories.

That's it.

If you're expecting *War And Peace* or the new Harry Potter, then trust me, you've got the wrong book. When my friends found out that I was writing a second book, a few of them asked me what it was about. Well, the truth is it's about nothing. Just stuff. Hopefully funny and interesting stuff, but stuff all the same. I like to see it as a great toilet book. Peruse a few chapters while having that satisfying toilet break in the day. Alternatively take this book away on holiday. You'll probably read the whole thing on the plane and be in a great and happy mood by the time you land. Maybe you're in jail. If so, why not use it to while away those empty hours? Then when it's finished, think about how to rehabilitate yourself back into society.

Either way, it's just a book of thoughts and stories and I hope you like it.

And, yes, I did write it myself, which is why there will probably be lots of spilling mestakes.

Chris Moyles, 2007

1

BREAKFAST HELL & BREAKFAST HEAVEN

I am moody in the morning. Proper moody. Grumpy might be a better word to use. I can't help it and I don't like it but I have to admit it. I am a grumpy bastard first thing. Always have been. I'm a night person and I like being a night person. Before I started working on the breakfast show for Radio 1, I was rarely awake before midday. Perfect.

These days my life is different. Luckily, when I began the morning show in January 2004, I was so excited that for the first few months I hardly even thought to moan about being up at 4.30am. As time passed the novelty of setting an alarm for five o'clock wore off, and now getting out of bed at 6.15am every morning is an effort. That said, my tolerance for the early hours has got better, and generally I do OK. Only occasionally will I upset somebody with my grumpiness.

Like last week. It was like going back to the days when I was Mayor of Grumpsville in the morning. I left my flat at 6.20am and walked through my gate to my waiting car. Anybody who has heard the show from the start at 7am will have no doubt heard me moaning about my car in the morning. Is it a Merc? No. Is it a limo? Not a chance. Does the driver wear a cap and a smart little uniform and call me 'Mr Moyles'? You've got to be kidding me. It took three years before I had a regular driver, and even now he might not be the one given the horrible job of picking me up. On this particular morning it was another guy. I walked through my gate and noticed that he was parked across the road outside somebody else's house.

'Moved, have I?' I said.

'Sorry, sir?' he politely replied.

'Well, I don't live here where you've parked so I must have moved.'

'Yes, sorry about that. I was going to park outside your house but there wasn't a space.'

'Fine. Whatever.'

It was at the moment I heard myself say 'Whatever' that I realised grumpy Chris was back in town. Who the fuck did I think I was? I only had to walk about ten steps across the road to a car that was waiting for me, and here I am being a twat to the driver, who incidentally has been there for ages because I'm ALWAYS late getting in my car. But it wasn't really me, it was grumpy me. I was actually appalled at how rude I was, and embarrassed too. When I got out of the car I tried to make it up to him by being extra nice when saying, 'Have a nice day, mate!' Like that didn't stop him from thinking: what a miserable arsehole. And why shouldn't he think that?

I WAS AN ARSEHOLE.

I know people who are grumpy in the morning, but it's OK because you know they are and you get used to it. But because I hid it for a while it surprises people when I am like that. I feel like some kind of druggie. I kept my secret for a while but now people were beginning to find out.

Some mornings I get to work and out of a list of fifteen things Rachel had to do the day before, there's one thing she hasn't done.

'Right, so you didn't actually do everything yesterday then?' Here I go again.

'No I didn't, but I was here till three and I should've left at one,' Rachel replies.

Do I really care about this one thing not being done? Will it ruin today's show? Of course it won't. And that's not what I'm trying to say. What I am saying is:

HELP ME! I HAVEN'T HAD ENOUGH SLEEP AND I CAN'T CONTROL BEING A GRUMPY BASTARD!

WELCOME TO OUR MORNING WORLD OF HELL.

But I'm not on my own. Dominic Byrne our newsreader, Carrie who reads the sport, Rachel our producer and Comedy Dave all have to get in BEFORE I DO, so every single day there's a room full of potential grumpy people who haven't had enough sleep. Because if your alarm goes off at 5.30am and you want eight hours' sleep, then you should really be in bed for 9.30pm. For me, this is virtually impossible. I don't know how the rest of the team do it. I don't get sleepy enough before that time at night. I'm only just settling down to watch TV.

I've always said it. If you want to be fresh in the morning and get up with no problems, then get to bed early. However, if you are going to start doing that, then say goodbye to your social life, your friends and most of your favourite TV shows. If you go out for dinner you'll be checking your watch all the time to see how late it is. Plus you can't travel far because if you go to a restaurant that's half an hour's drive away, you'll have to leave at least at 11pm if you want to be asleep before midnight, which is still only going to allow you five and a half hours' sleep.

I couldn't give up my social life because it would drive me insane, so I sacrifice my sleep instead. Hence, I'm often grumpy.

'So, what time are you up tomorrow?'

'Hey, shouldn't you be in bed now?'

'Hope you're going to get enough sleep tonight, Moylesy!'

I hear one or all of those every day. EVERY SINGLE DAY. It's like the world's most annoying catchphrase.

People ask me how I get up so early every morning. Well, it's hard enough for anybody who has to get up before 6.30am, I think. There are hundreds of thousands of people getting up a lot earlier than I do, and they probably hate their job. It's still quite hard for me cos I'm crap at getting up. The real answer is that you just have to. I appreciate how lucky I am because I LOVE my job. I don't like it, I LOVE it and that really helps. If I was putting the tops on tubes of toothpaste and had an alarm that went off every day at 5.30am, I wouldn't last a week. But I suppose with your dream job comes the downside, and getting up early is a massive one.

IT'S ROCK AND ROLL, BUT PLEASE BE IN BED BY 9PM.

So that's one question answered. Now I will run you through a typical day of doing our show and I hope that will answer any more questions you may have. (I sound like a waiter in a restaurant.)

My alarm is set for 5.30am. Each day Rachel (or Aled, depending on who is producing that day's show) will ALSO call me to wake me up. Now I know this sounds a bit extreme, and I don't think I'd fancy having to call somebody every day because they are too shit to be trusted to wake themselves up, but I *am* that bad at getting up. I often need several alarm calls, and if I've been out the night before and got in late, even more. I have woken up on more than one occasion to see eight missed calls on my phone.

When I eventually drag my fat arse out of the bed, I get showered and changed quite quickly. Then I pop my head into the bedroom and say goodnight to Sophie. I have to cos sometimes I won't see her until after seven o'clock that night. It's something I have done since the beginning, and it's quite cute I suppose.

Getting out of bed isn't the main problem, actually. Before that, I have to WAKE UP. Many mornings I answer the phone and go straight back to sleep. I don't mean to, I just can't help it. I get about five hours a night so I'm always knackered. On the whole I am a deep sleeper, but I can also wake up at the slightest thing.

Take, for example, a typical Saturday morning. Dave and I have always gone on about how much we LOVE Fridays. It's because you can do anything you like. You can go home after work and go straight to bed. If you sleep for six hours, it's not a problem because you don't have to be up early the next day. You can sit in the pub all day and get to bed at 2am and, again, it doesn't matter, because on Saturday I can wake up whenever I like. So most Saturdays Sophie wakes up before I do and knowing that I don't get enough sleep during the week, she'll leave me dozing for a while. I know that the job I do has given us both a nice life, but it can be hard for radio widows sometimes. Sophie could be a cow and wake me up when she gets bored, but she normally potters around the flat or gets some jobs done while I'm out of the way. One of these jobs might be putting away all the clean clothes. She'll sneak into the bedroom and open the drawer to put some socks in, and, guess what, I bloody wake up. I could sleep through an earthquake, but on a Saturday morning, open the sock drawer and I'm up like a shot!

It's sod's law that Monday to Friday I need an earthquake to wake me. I've tried so many types of alarm that I'm almost an expert on the subject. For example, I've tried setting my phone to a TV show theme tune that connects with my brain and wakes me up. But what actually happens is Sophie will nudge me saying, 'Why is the theme tune to *The Sooty Show* playing?'

I changed it once to the *Top of the Pops* theme tune. Sophie had been working on *Top of the Pops* for a good few years and she loved her job – that was, until the show got cancelled and they took it off the air. I suppose it wasn't the most sensitive piece of music to play at 5.30am when your girlfriend has just lost her job from the show!

After this I tried waking up to the radio, but I found that when I listened to the music and the DJs talking, I thought it was part of my dream. For three weeks I was really concerned because I thought I'd been dreaming about JK and Joel every night. Then I changed the radio to the 'buzzer' setting. This was very annoying for a while and then I got used to that sound too. Worse, I could unplug the clock radio in my sleep. I'd wake up late, as usual, wondering how the hell the plug had fallen out of the socket again.

Eventually I tried an old-fashioned wind-up clock. You know, the ones with the two bells on top. I went into my bedroom one night, set the alarm for 5.30 and wound the clock up. Then I placed the ticking clock right next to the bedroom door, thinking that when it went off, I'd have to get my arse out of the bed to switch it off, and then I'd be up and could walk straight into the bathroom and jump into the shower.

Incidentally, why do people use the word 'jump' when talking about getting in the shower? I don't think I've ever 'jumped' into a shower. It's more of an 'open the door and walk in' situation. And besides, surely it would be a health and safety issue if you did actually jump in?

Anyway, the next morning the alarm went off and it was very loud. I was obviously in a deep sleep and it woke me right up. I found myself leaping out of bed to switch it off. Brilliant. It had worked. I had finally found a way to get myself out of bed in the morning. Later that day, when Sophie came home from work, I still was so excited that I explained to her what had happened and how pleased I was.

'Well congratulations,' she said. I didn't think it warranted sarcasm. This was a big thing for me.

That night before we went to bed I wound up the clock and put it by the bedroom door.

'What are you doing?' asked Sophie.

'I'm setting my clock for the morning. It's brilliant,' I replied, and got into bed.

We lay there silent for about twenty seconds, then Sophie said, 'What the hell is that noise?'

'It's the clock ticking.'

'Oh I can't have that,' she moaned.

'What do you mean you can't have that?' I'd at last found a sure-fire way to wake up and here was Sophie moaning because it bloody ticked.

'I'm not going to be able to sleep with that thing ticking away all night long.'

'It's got to bloody tick, it's a clock for Christ's sake.' I wasn't daft. I knew how these things worked.

'Well, you're going to have to put it outside the room or I'm not going to get any sleep tonight with that thing.'

'That thing is meant to wake me up so there's not much point in putting it outside the bloody door, is there?' But by this point I knew I was fighting a losing battle.

'Well, I'm sorry but you'll have to find something else. It's way too loud.'

'It's a tick-tock noise, not a bloody explosion.'

I'd like to tell you that we argued for a while until I explained to her that I was an important man and if I didn't wake up in time millions of people around the world would miss my show and be in a bad mood all day, and that Sophie had to realise that although she would find it hard to sleep, she had to like it or lump it because the clock was staying.

Obviously I didn't.

'OK, FINE. Have it your way.' And I got out of bed and put the clock in another room.

I then reset my mobile phone to wake me up at 5.30am to the theme tune of *Top of the Pops*. Revenge is childish but sweet!

On a very rare morning that I do get up early I'll take a shower and get changed and stick the radio on while I tuck into a delightful bowl of Special K or Bran Flakes. This happens about once every six months. Most mornings I'm late and in a rush and I can just about have a wash and get my clothes on before I'm out the door.

Then it's into the car and off we go.

The ride only takes about ten minutes as I live quite close to the studio and there's little or no traffic at that time. Once at work, it's into our office and a quick chat with Dave and Rachel about last night's TV or what we have on the show today. Rachel is more often than not at her desk doing something or other – I've never really asked – and Dave is normally writing the Tedious Link feature for nine o'clock. Dave always writes this first thing in the morning, right before the show starts. I'd like to think he does this so he can make it topical, but I think it's just habit.

Then I head downstairs to the studio via our really groovy spiral staircase. In the middle room between all the studios I'll find Dominic and Carrie writing their News and Sports bulletins. Sometimes I'll pop in to see JK and Joel, who are on before us, but most days I don't. The reason I use for not going in to say hello to them is time. The truth is that JK and Joel fart so much during their show that their studio stinks. Sometimes one of them might have had a few beers the night before so it will smell of stale ale. Occasionally one of them won't have showered so there will be a slight smell of body odour. On a bad day, more often than not, the studio smells of a mixture of all three, and quite frankly, much as I love those boys, it's way too much to experience first thing in the morning.

One of my favourite things every day is walking into our studio. I still get a kick out of it. It's the biggest studio of three in the Radio 1 basement. A huge RADIO 1 logo is illuminated on the wall, and the actual radio desk where I work is huge and is split into two. One side is for Dave and Dom and Carrie, the other for me, where I press all the buttons. I always stand up. I find it keeps me awake and alert throughout the three hours we are on air.

Rachel runs me through anything I need to know for that day, and then we are live at seven o'clock.

Every day the show is different so it's hard to run you through what happens in any one show. What does happen regularly is promotion companies will send people or products, or both, to our studio in the hope of us talking about them. The items vary a lot. It might be donuts for National Donut Week. Or it might be orange juice. Or something random like a basket of paint samples and a teddy bear.

If we have a guest in that morning, they will normally turn up at about 7.40. They sit in the Live Lounge on the other side of the glass and Rachel briefs them on the show. Most guests know all about us, though some Americans need to be told which one is Dave and which one is me! I also have a very odd thing with the guests. If I have met them before, I normally say hello to them during a record. But if it's a new guest, I don't, leaving it until we are live on the air before we meet. Many DJs would do this the other way round, but not me. Also, unlike pretty much every other radio show in the world, our guests are walked in to the studio live. Most DJs would bring them in and sit them down during a record, but I like to get them in live. They do it on TV shows: as soon as the guests walk out they know they are on the show. And we do it too. Occasionally a guest doesn't realise we are live. They think we're idly chatting before we switch the micro-phones on. Wrong! We're already mid-link by the time they have opened the door to walk in. This gets a great natural reaction from our guests and means they're not as guarded as they might normally be.

When you're in the studio, the show goes very quickly.

Dominic and Carrie don't sit in the on-air studio for the whole show but are visible through the glass in the studio next door, so if I ever want them for a link about something or a game of Guess Who?, they can run in and join us live on air.

As much as we plan certain items, most things on the show just happen. I'm lucky that the team around me are VERY good at reacting to this. They can find pieces of music in seconds or go and record a phone call with somebody. Sure we have our set features that we know that we're going to do, but the really fun stuff is spontaneous. It's great fun to finish a show and look back and say:

'Well, I never thought we'd be speaking to Paul Daniels today.'

Or:

'I never knew Dominic could impersonate Frankie Dettori so badly.'

A lot of mornings when we reach the end we could keep on going. Before you know it, it's ten o'clock and we have to say goodbye and hand over to Jo Whiley in the other studio. In the old days you couldn't see who was on after you, but now we have a camera in each studio so we can watch a big screen and wave or flick the V sign at each other.

At ten o'clock the studio is bombarded with people for our after-show meeting. There will be somebody from the press, a person from our website, the guy who makes the daily advert for the show and the entire team including the day producer and assistant. (I'm trying my best to make this boring meeting sound quite cool!) We discuss the day's show and what we're going to do the next day.

After that it's normally another meeting with just myself, Dave, Aled and Rachel, where we talk about future Radio 1 things and what our show can do to get involved, or, as is sometimes the case, how we can get out of doing something we don't wanna do!

And that is pretty much it. Of course, there's a little more to it than that but I'm not going to give away all our secrets. I'm not an idiot. I've got a business to run here.

Just as the show is always different, no day is ever really the same. One morning I might be on my way home by 11.30am. Another day I might be sitting in the studio recording a new song parody. I love doing these because I sit in the studio on my own and sing like an idiot. I record the vocal, and then I add backing vocals. Honestly, I'm like a shit Simon Cowell!

Is it everything I thought it would be? I have to say yes. In fact, it's all and more. I love it. It's so much fun. I love the fact that we all laugh every single morning. I love the fact that Dominic and Dave make me laugh every day. I love the fact that when you're talking about an old TV show or a song from ages ago, the audience react instantly and text in to say that they remember it too. I love the fact that when you dare admit something embarrassing, the audience, or at least some of them, will admit they do exactly the same thing. Even when Dominic admitted to sitting on the toilet and talking out loud as he made up adverts for things he could see in the bathroom, like towels or hot water! Even when I admitted to walking around my flat and talking to myself when I'm on my own. Instantly the texts come in from people saying, 'I thought I was the only one who did that!' I also love the fact that I can spill my guts out over whatever it is that's winding me up that day. I can talk about anything. If I've got a problem with one of the team, then we can talk about it. Friends or family, it doesn't matter, I can get it off my chest live on the air. It's like being paid to sit on a psychiatrist's couch. All the things that I can't say out loud in real life, I can say on the air, and I bloody love it!

Since we started the show in January 2004, it has been the most enjoyable thing I have ever done. It's the most fun and I feel honoured to do it. It has opened up a whole world of opportunity not only to me, but to the rest of the team as well. After less than four years on the air, the show has increased its audience by over 1.75 million listeners, from six and a half million to over eight million. And it has changed all of our lives. Even when you forget about work and you're getting ready to go out, something will happen because of the show. One Saturday night Sophie and I were staying in the Malmasion Hotel in Oxford with a couple of friends of ours, Jamie and Vicky. The hotel is in the old prison and the rooms are the old cells. It's really quite cool. I was in the bathroom shaving before we went out for dinner and Sophie was lying on the bed watching TV. All of a sudden, she shouts at the top of her voice:

'CHRIS! QUICK!'

Jesus Christ, what was wrong? Had she hurt herself? Was there a ghost of a former inmate floating around the room?

No, none of those.

'Listen!' she said, pointing at the television.

There was David Gest sitting on the judging panel of *Grease is the Word* on ITV. He was talking about somebody and saying, 'If you're watching, Chris, don't change this channel, buddy. I love you, Chris. I love you, man.'

'What's that about?' I asked.

'It's you. He was talking about you. He said you bought him a clock radio in the shape of a crucifix or something.'

So there I was, stood in an old prison cell with a face half full of shaving foam and half full of beard, as Liza Minnelli's ex-husband was saying something about me buying him a present.

And it's all thanks to three hours on Radio 1 every morning.

We have an audience of over eight million people, and as much as there are many people who hate my guts, I know that for millions the show is an absolute must first thing in the morning, and that makes me very proud. Seriously it does. People tell me how much they love the show and though I get embarrassed, it is such a cool thing to hear. Especially as we all work so hard to achieve it.

It's a strange life, but I wouldn't have it any other way.

2

WHAT'S IT LIKE BEING FAMOUS?

This is probably the question I get asked the most, and if I'm honest with you, which I always am, it's also probably the question I hate being asked the most.

It's funny. You know, when people meet me they react in one of a few ways. Some people are very polite and will wait for a moment when I'm not too busy before they approach me. Often I'm with friends so they will walk up to us and wait before saying 'Excuse me' and apologising for interrupting.

THESE PEOPLE I LOVE.

They can approach me all the time and I have absolutely no problem with it whatsoever. And why would I have a problem with it, you might be asking. Well, it's simple. Even after being on Radio 1 for ten years, I still have a problem with being recognised. I'm embarrassed by it. Because it IS embarrassing sometimes. Imagine sitting in Pizza Express with your girlfriend and some stranger walks past the table and says something random about *your* life.

'Don't be up late tonight and be too tired in the morning for work!'

If that happened to you you'd probably tell them to piss off and mind their own business. You're a grown-up and can do what the hell you want!

For me, there are many problems associated with being recognised.

PROBLEM NUMBER 1.

The main problem is that I don't really think I am famous. Sure I'm on the radio every morning to eight million people, but that's the point, I'm on the radio. I'm not on TV every night of the week like those poor bastards in *EastEnders* or *Coronation Street*. These people are in your home every night of the week and are so recognisable it must be impossible for them to walk down the street without somebody staring at them. And I have met some famous people, and some not so famous, who absolutely LOVE to be recognised. Their career is fuelled by them being recognised in the street or stopped and asked for an autograph or a photo. But for me, that was NEVER part of the job. All I wanted to do was be on the radio. I wanted to have the number-one radio show in the country, but I never thought that with that you also become famous. I really didn't. And before you start thinking I'm talking bullshit, it's true. Here is the simple equation:

Radio doesn't make you famous. Television does.

And there's a big difference between being famous and being recognisable. I know actors who have been in loads of different TV shows playing a range of characters but they're not known for one thing so they don't often get spotted when they're out. Then I know other actors who have had just one job playing the same part, and these guys get stopped EVERY time they leave the house. So I never associated recognisable figures with famous figures.

Sure there are people who listen to my show every single day and feel part of our radio family. The 'die-hard' listeners I call them. I love these people. These people keep me going on the radio every single morning, because if it wasn't for them, what would be the point? Now of course I understand that if the 'die-hard' audience see me or somebody else from our show out in the street or in a bar one night, then they want to come over and say hi. They're excited to meet us and that's cool. But when it comes to making somebody instantly recognisable and indeed famous, Television is King.

Here's an example of how powerful a medium television is.

June 2006. I am the host of the Radio 1 Breakfast Show and have been for two and a half years. I have been on national radio for nine years and have millions of people listening to my show. I can walk down the street in London and occasionally somebody will say hello or shout 'Moylesy' out of a passing van window. Cool. Then I agree to sing on *X Factor – Battle of the Stars*. It goes out every single night on ITV for a week and I end up finishing third. Cool. Then I head out to Germany for the World Cup (for work!) and then have a holiday straight after that. When I return to Radio 1 and walk down the street after my first show back, I am amazed to see so many people recognising me and shouting stuff.

'You were robbed, Moylesy.'

'Sing us a song, Chris!'

'What's that Simon Cowell like in real life, Moylesy?'

'Hey, Chris, great show today. Love your singing voice too!'

I was amazed. There were many people who knew who 'Chris Moyles' was, and now they knew what I bloody looked like too. Most of these people who shouted stuff had probably driven past me a hundred times before but never noticed me. Now, because of the wonderful world of television, they notice.

So, despite not really wanting to be, I am, I suppose, if I have to admit it, in certain circles, kind of, semi-famous.

Now I've often said that I have a radar for spotting famous people, so I understand that I'll get recognised. As I've also said, people who are polite are cool. But often you get people who are not so polite, and these bastards are something else.

CUE PROBLEM NUMBER 2.

Sophie and I have come to the conclusion that because they think that I'm rude on the radio, then I'm going to be rude to them in real life too. So if they approach me, they feel the need to be rude first, before I am.

'All right, Moylesy, ya fat bastard!'

That's a fairly regular one. Or:

'Oi, say something funny then.'

That's always a weird one. I mean, what can you say apart from:

'Erm, how about fuck off, ya ugly twat?'

(I did respond once with that line and the fella wasn't laughing afterwards.)

Now this might happen if I'm on my own, or it could happen when I'm with friends. Once or twice it has happened when I've been with my dad, and, trust me, you don't want to be saying things like that when he's around. Remember, he was called Chris Moyles before I was and he doesn't like being called a fat bastard.

So you get some people who are polite, and some people who are twats. After that is the most random group. These are people who have recognised me but they don't want to say so. They do, however, want to say something, but they feel that, 'Are you Chris Moyles?' is somehow not the right thing to say. So instead – and I have no idea why they do this – they speak in code.

PROBLEM NUMBER 3.

Sometimes the code is easy to understand.

'Haven't you got to be up early in the morning? Eh!'

Simply translated, that means:

'I know you're Chris Moyles and that you have a radio show in the morning and I wanted to let you know that I knew this.'

Thank you. That's very kind of you.

Sometimes the code is more difficult to crack.

'Does Rachel know you're drinking tonight? Eh!'

Again, the translation is the same. They have recognised me as the host of a radio breakfast show and they also know that 'Rachel' is the producer of the show, and is she aware that I am drinking in a pub the night before? Gotcha!

The third type of code is very strange and can take a while to work out. They speak the code, but it doesn't have any relevance to where I am or what I am doing. However, its meaning is the same as the two previous cases. The most recent example of this was when me and Sophie were sitting on a shuttle bus going from the airport car park to Heathrow Terminal 4. A smart man in his late forties jumped on the bus and sat across from us.

'Excuse me, but did you remember what bit of the car park we got the bus from? I forgot to note it down,' said the nice man.

'Yeah, it was Row A, I think. Yeah, in fact, it was, because we got the bus at the first stop, so Row A, definitely,' said me.

'That's not what you said on Comic Relief!' The man looked at me and smiled.

What the fuck is he talking about? When did I say on Comic Relief that I was parked in Row Anything?

Of course I didn't say anything about where I was parked when I was on Comic Relief. What the nice man was saying was accurate. It was also code for: 'I know you're Chris Moyles and I recently saw you on the television on Comic Relief.'

THEN WHY DOESN'T HE JUST SAY THAT THEN?

Because that's just the way it is. Some people are polite, some people are rude and some talk in fucking riddles. It's all part of the job. And I'm kind of getting used to it. I mean I don't really have any choice.

I <u>HAVE</u> TO GET USED TO IT.

This really is now part of my job. When I started out on the radio I was a kid and I thought it was only about playing records and trying to make people smile, but these days there's way more to it than that. And it's not only me who has to deal with it. Sophie has to deal with it on an almost daily basis. Why? She's not famous. She's just a hot-looking blonde girl who happens to go out with a chubby DJ who gets recognised. And because of that, SHE gets recognised too. Well, when I say she gets recognised, it's mainly just because she is stood next to me. I can't tell you the amount of female friends who have been out with me some time and been asked: 'Are you the famous Sophie then?'

No, they're not. They're my friend that happens to be a girl. God forbid I ever try and have an affair; I wouldn't last five minutes before somebody comes up and asks if the girl I'm with is Sophie!

The reason people know her name is because I often talk about her on the radio show and bizarrely that has made her, dare I say it, slightly famous? It's so messed up, but it's part of my daily life.

Friends get caught up in it too. I'll be sitting having lunch with a friend or go and meet some friends for drinks. I might not have seen these people for a long time and I'm really looking forward to catching up with them. We sit down and start talking when suddenly somebody will come up and want a photograph or an autograph or something. Now as I've said, I don't mind it, I just get embarrassed over it. I'm not at work in the studio, yet I have to adopt my on-air persona and try to be the Chris Moyles these people want to meet, while at the same time trying not to freak my friends out by having a conversation with a total stranger when we're trying to eat pizza and catch up with each other.

I just wanna pause at this point and explain to you that I really don't mind all of this. I don't wanna come across as a miserable bastard who just wants to be left alone.

Obviously I AM a miserable bastard who just wants to be left alone, but the reason I'm telling you all this is because I want you to try and understand what it's like.

I really, honestly, never thought that my life would be like it is. I said before that I never wanted to be famous, but that isn't entirely true. I will now try and explain and be as honest as I can with you.

When I was younger, yes, I did want to be famous, but I didn't really know what 'being famous' was. And now that I have a certain amount of fame, it's hard to deal with it. Remember, nobody teaches you this shit: you just have to learn it. You quickly learn that if you're short or rude to somebody, they will go away and tell lots of their friends what a miserable bastard you are. Therefore you have to be nice to pretty much everybody. Now, of course, if somebody is drunk and rude I don't just sit there and take it, but every time I meet somebody it has an effect one way or another and I want people to think I'm a nice guy – because I am a bloody nice guy!

So **YES** when I was younger I thought I wanted to be famous, but not the famous that exists today.

You know when you watch *Big Brother* on the TV and these losers come on and say how they want to be famous. You know the kind of people I'm talking about. You sit on your couch and watch them, then you remark to the person sitting next to you, 'What a tosser.' Those people. Well, they actually want to be a 'celebrity'. These days being a 'celebrity' doesn't necessarily mean having a skill or being good at something. I knew from an early age what I wanted to do and I feel as lucky as hell that I got to be able to do it. Now, as I said, with that comes a certain amount of fame, but celebrity, I don't really go in for that. You won't see me walking down the red carpet at a movie premiere, or hanging out with footballers and page 3 models at the newest trendy club in London. Fuck that. That stuff isn't real and it's boring as hell.

Sure, when I started at Radio 1 and I got invited to a movie premiere, I went! Of course I did, who would turn that down? But I quickly realised that most of the people who turn up at these events are only trying to get photographed so they can be in the papers the next day. They don't give a shit about the movie, and some of them walk out after five minutes and don't even watch the thing. Once they've been photographed and flashed their legs at the camera, they're gone. Probably to China Whites to hang out with footballers and page 3 girls. No, that life is not for me, and I do everything I can to avoid it. I'll admit sometimes it's nice to play that role, like if Jon

Culshaw and I go to some event, it's quite funny to walk down the red carpet and take the piss out of each other, but mostly I'd rather stay in and watch TV or meet my friends in my local pub.

What I'm trying to say is that I feel like an ordinary bloke. I don't feel famous and therefore I'm not good at being famous. I know some famous people who are so good at being stopped in the street and asked for an autograph. They're so polite and funny. I just get embarrassed. One of the reasons I suppose is that I don't always understand why these people approach me. Let me explain.

A typical example of what happens is when I walk into a pub. Somebody will look at me, and then the look turns into a stare. Now, I've noticed this. Trust me, it's hard not to notice somebody staring at you while you're trying to order a pint. Then they will turn to the person they're with and whisper in their ear. I know that what they're saying is either:

'That's Chris Moyles.'

Or:

'That's that fella off the radio.'

Then their friend will turn and look in my direction and either mouth the word:

'Where?'

Or more embarrassingly:

'Who?'

This happens A LOT. In fact, I'm writing this in my room on holiday (deadlines and all that) and this just happened about five minutes ago!

Then there are autographs. I think sometimes people feel they should ask for an autograph as proof that they have met somebody famous. But where do these autographs live? I have signed beer mats, cigarette packets, bus tickets, all sorts of crap. Do these people keep these things? Does somebody actually have a scrappy piece of paper with my signature hurriedly written down on it sitting proudly on his or her mantelpiece? Well, yeah, they probably do. And I'm just as sad. Somewhere I've still got a napkin with the signature of Roger Taylor the drummer from Queen on it. I've also got a signed Hue and Cry album, a signed doll of Baby Spice Emma Bunton, and a framed, signed Leeds United shirt from the days when they were good.

WEIRD THINGS PEOPLE SAY WHEN THEY MEET ME.

There are many, and they are all true. Here are some of my favourites.

1. 'I went to school with you.'

I was raised as a Roman Catholic and I went to three different schools. I remember some people from my time there, but not all of them, so there is a good chance that when I'm in Leeds and somebody says that to me, it might be true. But normally it isn't.

'Oh right, which class were you in?'

'Well, I wasn't in the same year but it was the same school.'

'Oh, so you never actually went to school with me then?'

Or this one:

> 'I went to school with you.'
>
> 'Oh right, which school was that?'
>
> 'Corpus Christi,' they'll say proudly.
>
> 'I never went to that school, mate.'
>
> 'Yes you did!' they say angrily.

This really happens. Some people will tell me that I never did go to my school, but I went to their school instead.

2. 'Are you famous?'

This one kills me. I'm no psychologist, but if they have to ask if I am famous, doesn't that mean that no, I'm not? Also, what do they expect me to say? Should I fling back my long flowing hair, take a drag on my cigarette and declare in a posh English accent:

'Yes, dear man, I am indeed a famous person. Please back away and worship me from afar!'

3. 'You're Johnny Vegas, aren't ya?'

I don't mind this one because I think Johnny Vegas is funny, and you can tell when somebody asks me this that they like Johnny Vegas. I do worry, though, that as I'm stood in a pub somewhere trying to convince somebody that I'm not Johnny Vegas, he's across London in a different pub trying to explain to somebody that he isn't Chris Moyles.

4. 'Will you say hello to me on the radio?'

This again is a strange one and I will be very honest with you: if I am in a pub on a Friday night and I have had a few to drink, then the answer is NO. I'm not being rude, but the chances of me remembering on Monday morning that at 7.25 I have to say hello to Tommo, Robbo and Bobbo who I met over fifty hours ago while I was drunk, are very slim. People ask me to say hello to them on the radio, and I say, 'Yeah sure,' and then they give me a list of about eight of their mates. If you ever see me in a pub on a Friday night and do this to me and I say I'll say hello to all of them, I'm afraid I'm lying and you will be disappointed.

I must say though, even after everything you have just read, that it is a nice, fulfilling feeling when somebody wants to say hello. Remember, all I ever wanted to do was be on the radio and make people laugh. The team I put together and now work with every morning feels like a family and I genuinely believe we have a radio show that people can not only relate to or really get into, but can also love. And they do. They don't just like us, they LOVE us. Isn't that what it's all about? So when people want to come up and say hi, I see it as reminder that what we do in our little studio every day means enough to somebody that they want to meet me. Or Aled, or Dominic or Comedy Dave. They hear us every day and feel they know us enough to say hello. And that is an amazing and very cool thing.

So – thank you. I really mean it.

Just leave me alone when I'm wolfing down a pizza!

NORMAN COOK ON MOYLES

1. Before I met Chris I thought he was an arrogant fat fuck. Since getting to know him I've realised first impressions can be wrong...

2. Chris is undoubtedly the second-best breakfast presenter Radio 1 has ever had, a dear personal friend and I cannot fault him except for his choice in football team and of course the constant verbal abuse he has given me over the years.

3. The only reason that me and Zoë had a son was to give me the motivation to get up early and actually listen to Chris's show on the school run.

4. To be a guest on Chris's show is sublime, to hear him play the cuíca is divine, to go drinking with him is dangerous but very entertaining and to watch him squirm sitting next to me as the Seagulls beat Leeds is a joy rarely known to mortal man.

COMIC
RELIEF

I've always liked Comic Relief.

The idea that you can spread awareness and raise money for worthy causes while having a laugh is brilliant. The balance between videos of orphaned children in the slums of Africa and Dawn French having a snog with Hugh Grant works well and makes a lot of money. Back in 1988 when the first Red Nose Day hit our screens, it raised £15 million, and to date well over £400 million has been raised.

In 1994 I was working in Stoke-on-Trent. This was heavily detailed in my first book and I don't wish to remind myself of it. No offence to the people of Stoke, you're OK, but generally it is an odd place. Come to think of it, I have spent quite a bit of my time as a travelling DJ in 'odd places', including Milton Keynes and Dunstable. Hardly New York and Milan. Anyway, back in 1994 in Stoke-on-Trent, I worked with a guy called Spence. He presented the breakfast show; I did the evening show. We were similar in many ways:

He liked a drink, and so did I.

He had a bitchy sense of humour, and so did I.

He was tubby, and so was I.

Through a friend of mine called James we managed to get ourselves a pair of tickets to sit in the audience on Red Nose Day at BBC Television Centre in London. I was SO excited as I'd never been there before. (I still get a buzz every time I go through the gates and up to what is known as the 'stage door'.) We drove down to London, full of anticipation.

Which top celebrities will we see?

Will we meet any famous celebrities?

Will we get into the party afterwards?

What time will that finish?

HANG ON A SECOND.

How will we get home if we've both had a drink?

Shit!

Where are we gonna stay?

Double shit!

Where the fuck are you meant to park in London, I've been driving round for half an hour?

Triple shit and bugger!

The show was broadcast live at seven, it was now 6.45 and we were still trying to park. We got lucky and found the one remaining parking space in Shepherd's Bush. That's a place in London, by the way – not to be confused with an STD for people who look after sheep. We dumped the car, raced into Television Centre and took our seats in the studio. The host for the first hour was Chris Evans. At the time I really liked Chris Evans. He was an original broadcaster with a nod of respect for the old-school DJs. He was fresh, talented and very funny. The show was the usual funny Comic Relief stuff and, before we knew it, it was nine o'clock and the show took a break for the news. The audience were thanked for their support and then turfed out to make way for a fresh new audience that had been waiting outside.

Now, Spence and I had been promised tickets for the after-show party, which we hadn't received. We were told not to worry, we'd be on the guest list. You might think it strange that there is a party for Comic Relief. After seeing the show first-hand, I can tell you that A HELL OF A LOT OF WORK goes into a seven-hour virtually non-stop broadcast, so why shouldn't they have a little party afterwards? You what? Because they're meant to be raising money for people who need it, not spending it on getting pissed? I see your point, but at the same time they DO raise a lot of money for people who need it, and then some of them get pissed, so back off!

We made our way to the 'stage door' bit of Television Centre. (Television Centre is known in the Beeb as T.V.C. They like abbreviations there. Broadcasting House is B.H. In fact I heard someone at Radio 1 refer to me as F.A.T. – whatever that means.) As we approached the reception area, I saw two women sitting at a table. A note on the table read 'Comic Relief Guest List'.

'That'll do us,' said Spence, already looking forward to his liquid reward after sitting in a studio audience for two hours.

As we got nearer, I noticed a man arguing with one of the women behind the desk.

'But my name is meant to be on the list, check it again.'

'Sorry, sir, but I have checked and your name isn't down on this list. I can't let you up there,' said the nice lady.

I realised that our names were probably not on that list either, and that in a few seconds that nice lady would be throwing Spence and me out of the building too. So I thought on my feet, and using my quick reflexes and imagination, I decided there and then:

THAT WE WOULD LIE OUR WAY INTO THE COMIC RELIEF PARTY.

OK, so I'm not proud of it, but what would you have done?

As we approached the desk I looked up to see the lifts to the other floors, and to my amazement, a sign next to one of the lifts read:

COMIC RELIEF PARTY 6th FLOOR

'Spencer, I have an idea,' I proclaimed.

'What?' asked Spencer, reasonably enough as he didn't know what it was yet.

'My old man has always said that if you look like you know where you are going, nobody will question you. As long as we look confident enough, we can get in that lift and ride it up to the sixth floor, then blag our way into the party and hang out with Vic and Bob. Easy.'

'Sounds good to me,' said Spence, by now ready for a drink.

So we bypassed the nice lady at the desk and walked straight up to the lifts. As we got there, some people were just getting in.

'Hold the lift please,' a voice said. It was mine, cocky git. I'm not meant to be here and I'm asking somebody who really works here to hold the lift open for me and my mate so we can bluff our way into a party and drink for free. The shame of it.

Anyway, it worked, and before we knew it we were on the sixth floor.

I'll admit that drinking free booze laid on for genuine BBC staff who had been grafting their asses off to raise money for starving kids, while me and my mate had driven down from Stoke and hadn't raised any money for Comic Relief whatsoever, may have been a wee bit cheeky. To make matters worse, a television in the corner of the room was showing videos of starving kids. With all this in mind, I opted for water and tried to look all charity like. Spence meanwhile found his first free bottle of Becks.

The room was packed full of top celebrities. There was Vic Reeves and Jonathan Ross in one corner. Lenny Henry in another. Even HRH Prince Andrew was in the room, although I never saw him wearing a red nose and doing something silly. (He normally didn't need a red nose for that.)

Spence and I thought this was an opportunity not to be missed, and after thinking what we could do to meet some of our comic heroes, we opted for getting everybody to sign a bit of the night's script so that we could give it away. By 'give it away' we meant 'keep for ourselves'. Kathy Burke signed it, as did Angus Deayton. Then I decided to go and speak to one of my personal comedy heroes, Vic Reeves. I wandered into the corner and politely waited for him and Jonathan Ross to stop talking and notice me.

'Hello young man,' said Vic Reeves, TO ME!

'Hi. My name is Chris Moyles and I was just wondering if you would sign this bit of script for me, please,' I whimpered.

As Vic was signing it, I was overcome with a ridiculous urge to explain I was a big fan of his work. How much I'd loved *Vic Reeves' Big Night Out* and also *Shooting Stars*, which had aired just the once as a special on BBC TWO. I tried to explain all that, but failed.

'I just wanna say how much you inspire me to be funny and that you're great!' I was pathetic.

Then I made it worse.

'I'm going to write a brilliant comedy one day and it's gonna be great and when I do, I'd love you to be in it. Would you be in it?'

I was shot down in flames by a young Jonathan Ross.

'*NO. FUCK OFF!*' yelled Jonathan.

Charming. Although I can't say I blamed him and, besides, I wasn't meant to be in that room in the first place. To my surprise Vic just smiled and asked me what the comedy show would be about.

'Oh I don't know yet cos I haven't written it, but I will do one day and I would love you to be in it cos you're great and all that.' Jesus I was such a loser.

'Well, if you write it and somebody makes it, and it's funny, then sure I'll be in it,' said Vic Reeves, TO ME.

Suddenly Jonathan changed his tone. 'Yeah yeah and I'll do it as well.'

This was becoming one of the most surreal nights of my life. Prince Andrew in one corner, a TV showing starving kids in the other, and me and Vic Reeves discussing a part in my non-existent sitcom while Jonathan Ross told me to FUCK OFF.

I had tasted showbiz, and I wanted some more!

I said my thank yous and left them to their chat. In all my excitement I'd forgotten about Spence. By the time I found him, he was sitting on a sofa looking very drunk and tired from free charity-raising Becks. And when I say tired, I mean asleep!

I was very used to Spencer's drinking habits. In fact, I was too used to them.

'Spence, please don't be asleep, pal. We're in the BBC at a party we shouldn't be at. Spencer? Spencer, wake up. This could be very embarrassing for the pair of us. I really need you to wake up right now.'

'Fuck off,' he slurred.

I decided to leave him and go to the loo. He was out of it, so things couldn't get any worse.

On my return, things had got worse. Some pranksters had tied helium balloons to Spencer's head, placed a party hat on him and … WERE HAVING THEIR PHOTO TAKEN WITH HIM!

During all of this, Spence was STILL asleep.

'Dude, you gotta wake up now, pal, people are having their photo taken with you.'

He didn't wanna wake up.

'Hey, mate, can we stick some lipstick on him as well?' asked one of the hilarious photographers.

'No, you fucking well can't.'

I respected Spencer's dignity.

Eventually he woke up and asked why he had helium balloons tied to his head. I suggested we made our way to a hotel. Now, earlier on that night I had met Chris Evans. As I said, he was one of my heroes and I had been very excited to meet him. He and Spence had worked together in Manchester.

'You guys leaving already?' asked Chris.

'Yeah, we are, Spence is … tired. Hey, I don't suppose you know of any cheap hotels round here, do you?'

'Yeah, there's one round the corner I often use. Out of here, take a right, then left, then right at the roundabout.'

'Brilliant, thanks very much, Chris,' said a polite me.

'Mmmmmm,' said Spence.

We got in the car and followed Mr Evans's directions until we found the Hilton Hotel. It was when I was told how much it would be for a twin room that I realised famous people had more money than local-radio DJs, and that their idea of cheap wasn't mine.

'Fuck that, we can't afford that,' shouted Spencer. 'We'll find somewhere else. Come on.'

Find somewhere else – where? We were both in London, which we didn't know, on a Friday night, with no money, and one of us was drunk with helium balloons flying from his head.

We got back in the car and headed into the West End.

Now, as if free drink at the party for Comic Relief, which we weren't invited to, wasn't enough, it got worse. By the end of the night my morals were in tatters.

We found a hotel and decided we wouldn't be able to afford this one either. So we did something that we promised never to do again.

Spence had nicked Chris Evans's Comic Relief pass. It had 'Chris Evans' written on one side, and 'COMIC RELIEF' in big letters on the other. I put the pass round my neck and walked with Spencer into the posh hotel.

'Can I help you gentlemen?' asked the posh man behind the desk.

'Yeah sure. We have just finished working for Comic Relief on Red Nose Day down the road at the BBC. We have to be back in a few hours, at six in the morning, so we were wondering if you would be very generous and give us a room for a few hours to sleep in … for free.'

The posh man looked both of us up and down. 'Let me check with my manager.'

He disappeared into a small room. After a few seconds, he returned to the desk.

'My manager says you can't have it for free, but as it's for Comic Relief, you can have it for £30. Is that OK?'

Yeah, we had just blagged a posh hotel room in London for the night, and we used charity as our cover. Brilliant.

Incidentally I still haven't written my comedy yet, but when I do, my first phone call is to Vic Reeves.

It's partly because of all that, and also because of how much I genuinely love Comic Relief, that I am now so PROUD to be part of the Comic Relief extended family. It was in 2005 that we first decided to get involved and do our bit.

We had to come up with inventive ways of raising cash, and make it sound like a good laugh on the radio. On top of that, we wanted to get out on the road with something visually exciting. When we brainstorm ideas at work, we sometimes get carried away, and this is what we came up with.

The Chris Moyles Red Nose Rally. A week-long trip broadcasting live from all over the UK from John O'Groats to Land's End. Sounds like fun, right? But then we also needed ways of making money from it. So we hired a huge articulated lorry and stuck a picture of me down the side of it. For the launch of the breakfast show we had commissioned a caricature of me as Superman, so we stuck a red nose on it and reused that. The idea of the lorry was to blag as many brilliant prizes as we could, fill the truck on our travels and then give away the contents every day. This became the 'Truck of Luck'. Listeners had to text in an answer to a question and one lucky person won the lot. Seventy pence from each text went straight to Comic Relief and on to the Red Nose Rally total.

(Curiously, a children's BBC programme appeared later in the same year where Reggie Yates filled a truck with prizes and gave them away to one winner. The show was called *Mighty Truck of Stuff*. I'm assured this was purely coincidental. Whatever!)

So we had our prizes and a way of raising money from our audience – greed always seems to work in these cases – and now we needed corporate money from big companies. So it was decided that me, Comedy Dave, Rachel and Aled would 'whore' ourselves out to these companies in order to get more cash. If you wanted us to serve in your sandwich shop, it was gonna cost ya. If you wanted us to stop off at your workplace and say hello to everybody, it was gonna cost ya. This, although being a great idea to raise money, was one of the most tiring things I have ever done. In one day we would get up at 5.45am to get ready for the live radio show. When the show had finished at 10am we'd do interviews with the local press and pose with any listeners who wanted a picture – for money, of course. Then we'd get on to the tour bus (every tour needs a tour bus, right!) and travel to our next location, stopping to prostitute ourselves on the way. Pizza-making in one place, filling cream cakes in another, even bouncing on a trampoline while downloading an email from a wireless laptop. We were whores for charity. In the evening there'd be just enough time for a bite to eat and quick pint before heading to bed ready to do it all over again the next day.

So we had the live radio shows, the truck with the prizes, a big red tour bus and a host of companies begging to buy us for half an hour or so to do stupid shit, but it still wasn't enough. We needed an extra thing. Something that would grab people's attention as we drove across the country. Something that would make our presence known as the rally rolled into a new town or city. That's right, we needed replica cars from the movies and TV shows. And we got 'em. A few months beforehand I had found a website that provided such cars for corporate and private events. We called them up and they were only too happy to help. So here's what we ended up with.

First up was a DeLorean, the famous car that whisked Marty McFly *Back to the Future*.

Next was a Ford Gran Torino from *Starsky and Hutch*, complete with flashing red police light on top.

We also had *The A-Team* van, complete with the sliding door at the side; well, kind of, but more about that in a second.

Add to the list Comedy Dave's favourite vehicle, the General Lee from *The Dukes of Hazzard*, and yes it did have THAT horn.

And finally, my personal favourite, the *Knight Rider* Trans Am. That's right, KITT the car, complete with the front scanner light AND turbo boost buttons inside. Wicked.

So we now had everything we needed for a fundraising week on the road. The rest I have already written about in my diary, so as I'm too lazy to rewrite it, here it is!

DIARY OF A RED NOSE RALLY

Thursday 3 March 2005

We fly to Inverness and meet all the crew for our big rally. We see our tour bus for the very first time and meet the driver Dougie, who has been driving rock bands around for years. We haven't yet seen the cars. They will be at John O'Groats when we arrive tomorrow. After dinner in the hotel, we settled down to watch *Comic Relief does Fame Academy*, as my mate Jon Culshaw was singing on it. I say singing, but he sounded more like a bloke being strangled down a dark alley. I know it's for charity but Jesus Christ, I'd pay to STOP him singing. Bless him.

Friday 4 March 2005

Today was our first day on the road, well, kind of. We broadcast our show from the BBC studios in Inverness. (Is there anywhere the BBC don't have studios!) After a quick press call, we drove to a heliport where we all climbed into a helicopter to fly to John O'Groats. To say I was shitting myself would be an understatement. The pilot told us he did this trip several times a day, so at least he knew what he was doing. I'm sure we were told it was only going to take about twenty-five minutes. Anyway the weather was bad and it took about forty-five minutes. Rachel, my producer, was as cool as a cucumber as Aled and I held on for dear life. As we approached our landing site, the weather got worse, so the pilot decided it would be hilarious to drop us and the helicopter about thirty feet. What a joker he was and we all really appreciated the gesture. I made a gesture of my own as he flew off. When we landed, apart from looking happy because I was still alive, and happy to see that we had a crowd of people come to wave us off, I saw all our Star Cars together for the first time (minus the A-Team van which had been held up) and they looked wicked. The place itself was very odd. There is a 'Start' line, which says 'Finish' on the other side, this being for people who start at Land's End and finish at John O'Groats – who incidentally we never even got to meet. You'd have though this John fella would have popped out to say hello!

After avoiding a hailstorm of Flash Gordon proportions, we launched the start of our rally and jumped in a car each to set off back to Inverness, where we'd just bloody come from! We got round the first corner, and stopped in a car park.

'Why are we stopping here?' I asked Will Kinder, co-organiser of the tour.

'Well, we need to load the Star Cars on to the vehicle transporter.'

'And why would we need to do that?' I asked.

'Because basically these cars are for show only, and are not built to travel the distance we need them to, so to save them from breaking down, we're gonna stick them on the back of the transporter and drive the lot back to the hotel in Inverness.'

YOU'VE GOT TO BE KIDDING ME?

So we've hired a load of cars that can't drive down the road without breaking down? We're meant to be driving the length of the UK for Christ's sake and we can't even pass a car park without stopping. Will assured me that everything was fine and I should just get back on the tour bus and have a rest. This was easy to do. It had taken forty-five minutes to fly from Inverness to John O'Groats in a helicopter, but on the tour bus it was going to take us three hours to drive back. Brilliant. So here I am, sitting on a tour bus, driving back to where we started from, following a vehicle transporter that is carrying some famous movie cars, including one that is meant to be able to travel back in time, yet can't get back from John o'Groats. Maybe this isn't going to be as easy as I thought!

Saturday 5 March 2005

We started the day by taking the Star Cars to get washed and cleaned up. They did look wicked driving down the road in procession – that is, when they actually did drive! Then it was straight into 'whoring' ourselves out to raise some money. Aled and Rachel stopped off at a tanning place, where they picked up some cash and tried out some tanning products. They left the hotel this morning looking normal. They returned looking more orange than David Dickinson. Comedy Dave and I headed to Subway where we were asked to make a foot-long sandwich. (Things are already odd and we've only just begun!) Then we all headed to Glasgow where we had to do a trolley dash in a soft furnishing outlet. Apparently I wasn't allowed to put the till in the trolley, but we still made a nice bit of cash. In the evening we held a pop quiz and raised even more money. After that, we had a few well-earned beers and went to bed ... only to be woken up at six when the hotel fire alarm went off. We stood outside in the freezing cold for twenty minutes while the hotel made sure everything was safe inside. As we walked back inside, a member of the crew told me he thought it might have been his fault.

'What do you mean?'

'Well, I thought I'd fill a bath when I got back to my room, but I fell asleep and it overfilled,' he explained.

'Overfilled by how bloody much?' I wasn't impressed.

'By about an hour,' he replied.

I didn't talk to him any more after that. Idiot.

Sunday 6 March 2005

I started this morning by heading to the offices of the *Daily Record* to 'edit' their showbiz pages. It's easy. I've read showbiz pages before so I knew exactly what to do. I had a cup of tea and made some stories up.

After causing quite a decent traffic jam on the way to Edinburgh and stopping off to do another trolley dash, we ended up at the Edinburgh Dungeon, trying their new Mirror Maze. I know this was meant to be funny, but I kept walking into the bloody mirrors, and when you're wearing a red plastic nose, it begins to hurt after a while! We ended up in Newcastle in the early evening.

Monday 7 March 2005

After the show this morning from BBC Radio Newcastle, the A-Team van finally arrived. It looks brilliant and even has a sliding door on the side. We piled in ready to jump out for awaiting press photographers, but the bloody door got jammed and we ended up stuck in the back of the van for twenty minutes. A-Team my arse. Then it was more stupid things to do in Leeds, Manchester and Liverpool. I know we're raising a lot of money, but I'm shagged already and it's only Monday night.

Tuesday 8 March 2005

Ali Bastian, who plays Becca in *Hollyoaks*, was on the show today. Now she is gorgeous. Bit of a hooter on her, but hey, I'm not moaning. She was a good sport and went with Aled to play receptionist at our hotel to raise more money. Man, she looked fit in her receptionist outfit – all wasted on Aled, of course. Then we had a photo shoot at the Albert Dock with Rachel Stevens. I know she's meant to be really fit, but she's a bit boring. Give me Ali Bastian any day, even with the large conk. Later in the day I had to stop off at a school and read a story with the children's TV show character Brum. Brum is a radio-controlled car, so I didn't really have much support from him. He just moved back and forth and winked his headlight eyes at me. Dirty car! I've never read to a bunch of school children before, and even though I was told I did quite well, I don't think I should've told the kids I was shitting myself! After that I was told I wouldn't like the next job, but it would make us a nice wedge of cash for Comic Relief.

'I've just read stories to school children with Brum the car – it can't be much more embarrassing than that, can it?'

Well. It seems I had to go to Severn Trent sewerage works and clean out the filters. Yum yum. First I had to wear a luminous-green safety outfit. It didn't protect me, I could still smell the shit. Then I had to scrape the filters to remove any sewage caught up in them. Nice. All this while Chappers (he's the Comedy Dave of Scott Mills' show – but not as funny) and Comedy Dave watched on. They laughed through the whole thing. Bastards!

Wednesday 9 March 2005

Another day, another surreal set of fundraising activities. First up, tennis with gorgeous TV presenter Holly Willoughby. Fuck knows what that was for. Who cares anyway? She's well fit. From Cambridge we went to Slough and then to Bristol, where I met Nick Park and Gromit from Aardman Animations. They gave us a special framed drawing of Wallace and Gromit wearing red noses. Bless them. Then we ended up in Cardiff for the night. Now, I've been lucky enough to stay in many hotels around the world. Some rooms have had a plasma on the wall. Some rooms provide a full mini bar with a choice of snacks. I've even stayed in a room with free internet access, DVD player, games console AND a TV at the end of the bath so you can watch TV while you have a soak. So which of these did tonight's hotel have in the room? Answer, none of them. No TV. No mini bar. Not even a bloody phone. Not that it made much difference because there was no restaurant, bar or room service, so there was nobody to call anyway!

The good news is that we have almost raised half a million, which is amazing.

Thursday 10 March 2005

So far, since we started this rally, we have been to a fair few places.

John O'Groats

Inverness

Glasgow

Edinburgh

Newcastle

Leeds

Manchester

Liverpool

Birmingham

Coventry

Cambridge

Slough

Bristol

Cardiff

And we've raised half a million pounds for Comic Relief. So I was delighted to find out that today, from Cardiff, we were to head down to Exeter and then finally on to Land's End itself.

We were greeted at Land's End with a parade of fireworks, a steel band and a load of cheering people. The best sight though was the 'End to Enders' sign. I was now one of the lucky (and maybe slightly mad) bunch of people who had travelled from John O'Groats to Land's End and seen the sign at both ends. One by one we drove over the finishing line in our Star Cars. First was the General Lee, blasting out the famous horn that was once hilarious to hear but has now come to irritate us! Next was Knight Rider, followed by the Starsky and Hutch car, the A-Team van and finally our massive Truck of Luck. We signed the register, got our certificates and had our photo taken at the famous sign. As the sun shone down from the clear blue skies, we all felt we had achieved something. We were knackered, but we had raised a lot of money that would go on to save lives. We had done it. Our tour was almost at an end.

All we had to do was get into another helicopter and fly to Plymouth. This time, the British navy flew the helicopter. On the air earlier I had made the mistake of saying that we were to be flown by the army. This did not go down well with the navy boys, and they mentioned this to me about once or fifteen times. To hammer the point home, they decided to drop us, in the helicopter, like a lead balloon. I have now had two helicopter flights this week, and they have both dropped us for a laugh. Oh how fucking hilarious. Try telling that to my pants. We landed safely and found our hotel. We were all in need of a good drink and a nice rest, so were delighted to check into yet another hotel from the same chain as the night before. Who needs phones in their rooms anyway!

Friday 11 March 2005

Red Nose Day has arrived. After the show and a photo shoot in Plymouth, the rally headed back to London. We arrived at Radio 1 and realised we had some spare time until seven o'clock, when the Comic Relief TV show started, so Dave and I hijacked Pete Tong's radio show.

'It's the Crazy Frog for the next hour unless you text in.'

It worked, and we added the few final pounds to our grand total. By the time we arrived with our Truck of Luck and our Star Cars at BBC Television Centre, where incidentally we were met by Mr Lenny Henry himself, we had raised £628,282. Which doesn't look that big in digits, so try this. We raised:

SIX HUNDRED AND TWENTY-EIGHT THOUSAND, TWO HUNDRED AND EIGHTY-TWO POUNDS

Nice eh!

In 2007 we did ANOTHER rally. This time we travelled around the UK with our very own Chris Moyles karaoke show – obviously we called it the Chris Moyles Rallyoke. We did the radio show in the morning, and the live karaoke show at night. We also invited some special guests to perform with us, some of whom actually turned up and sang.

As you can imagine, tours like these are riddled with problems and need a lot of organisation and stroky-beard meetings. One of the first problems we encountered was who was going to work the karaoke equipment. We needed a person, or people, who knew how it worked and could look after it, so that it was one less job for the radio team to worry about. We also needed a warm-up act. Some person, or people, who could work the crowd up into a frenzy, but were also not as good as us, so that when we came on we got a big cheer. (Egos never stop you know, even at Radio 1.) After discussing certain possibilities, it came to our attention that Butlins was willing to help us out by providing some of their Redcoats. This wasn't the sexiest of ideas, but fuck it. We were desperate and they were free. So after careful consideration from Aled (Dave and I were way too busy to spend our afternoons picking giddy Redcoats), two eager young scamps were chosen to be our warm-up karaoke act.

Introducing Kim and Andy from Butlins, Bognor Regis. (I told you it wasn't very sexy, but Andy did win Entertainments Team Member of the Year for 2006. Bless him.)

Once these two were in place, we got our tour buses and our new Truck of Luck and headed out on the road for more money-raising. I really am very similar to Mother Teresa, only slightly taller and fatter.

The tour would take in Swansea, Liverpool, Belfast, Glasgow, Loughborough and then London, all in one week, with the radio show every morning. First stop was Friday night in Bournemouth, with special guests McFly. They sang 'Time Of My Life', which was very funny. Then we set Harry the drummer up to sing 'Hero' by Enrique Iglesias. He wasn't impressed but he did it all the same. This charity business is great for getting people to do stuff they don't really want to do.

In Swansea, Kelly Jones from the Stereophonics came along. We wanted him to sing, but at the last second he got nervous. It's a weird thing, you know. Sometimes performing on stage in front of thousands is easier than performing on stage in front of hundreds. Eventually we talked him into it … with vodka.

Liverpool was brilliant as loads of sexy famous women that I fancy turned up and they all wanted to duet with me. Get in!

First was Nikki Sanderson who played Candice in *Coronation Street*. I'd met her when I did *X Factor* so I knew she had a really nice singing voice. She is also very cute. Then it was the turn of Roxanne Pallett from *Emmerdale*. I didn't know beforehand if she could sing and quite frankly I didn't care. We did a duet of 'Endless Love' by Lionel Richie and Diana Ross. It's one of those slow love songs and all the way through Roxanne was looking into my eyes and being all sexy. Jesus this girl could act, I was all giddy by the end of it. Finally was the lady any man would love to have on stage on a charity karaoke night: Miss Gemma Atkinson. God knows what we sang but she looked good. Oddly, that night the girls were not the highlight of the evening. That honour went to my dad, the original Chris Moyles. I got him on stage to sing and the crowd went mental for him. When he finished the crowd cheered even more and I have to admit to being a bit emotional. From seeing him lying in hospital on his arse (he'd had a quadruple heart bypass a few years back and had recently been ill again) to seeing him on stage in front of a crowd of cheering people, it was a nice feeling.

By now it was Monday morning and after we did the radio show from Liverpool, we flew to Belfast to sing with Tim from the band Ash, and Mister Music himself, Louis Walsh. I'd never heard Louis sing before and I can now reveal that he was ... absolutely shite!

The next day and a flight to Glasgow, where we were honoured with songs from Scottish legend Fred MacAulay and then Travis front man Fran Healy, who dressed as Brandon from The Killers to perform one of their songs. Complete with fake moustache. At a karaoke night. I told you my life was surreal.

When we arrived in Loughborough we were all so tired. The late nights and the early mornings were taking their toll. However, the sight of Jo Whiley dressed as a nurse certainly helped wake me up. Sara Cox and Vernon Kay also came along and sang – if you can call it singing. Sara sounded like a bird being attacked by a fox!

Finally we arrived in London to perform at a place called Koko in Camden Town. I had only been there once before to watch Coldplay perform, so it was odd that my radio team and me would be filling the place to sing songs badly. For the London show we hired a band to play for us instead of karaoke CDs, and we organised quite a decent special-guest list as well. Brit nominee Jamelia was our first guest and she sounded amazing. Then we announced to the crowd our second guest: Mr Roy Walker. The crowd went mental for him. And he didn't disappoint us with his rendition of 'I'm a Believer'! After Davina McCall rocked out to Lenny Kravitz's 'Are You Gonna Go My Way' I thought the night had peaked, but it hadn't. Then it was Kelly Osbourne and myself singing 'I Got You Babe', followed by a very nervous looking Sarah Harding from Girls Aloud singing Oasis's 'Roll With It' with me. By the end of the night we had raised a lot of money and I had sung badly with even more famous women.

The next night it was over to Television Centre again to present Jonathan Ross with our total, which was £600,000. Though by the time they had counted up all the money from the week it was actually over £700,000. (God knows how you misplace a hundred grand. I mean, I've lost fivers down the couch before but that's just silly!) The nice thing about raising money like this is you notice how many people put their hand in their pocket. I don't mean metaphorically, I mean they stick their hand in their pocket and give us what they have.

We have to count all the money and bag it up. If you've ever saved loose change in a bottle or a jar, then you'll know how long it takes to get to £20. When you see every penny and every pound counted out in front of you, it really makes you appreciate just how much a hundred pounds is, let alone a hundred thousand. Even though we spent the week having a laugh, I was delighted with how much we raised.

I am amazed and blown away at the generosity of everybody we encountered on our rally. I am so proud of our audience for texting in and raising a lot of money.

All I have to do now is convince Richard Curtis that next time I can take just 5 per cent for my efforts!

As with a lot of things in life, there are perks to raising money for charity. For me it was a chance to be on stage with Matt Lucas from *Little Britain*.

I was asked if I would take part in a sketch for a gala night of their *Little Britain Live* tour, with all the proceeds going to Comic Relief. Loads of famous faces were going to be involved, from the likes of Peter Kay, Jonathan Ross and Russell Brand to Patsy Kensit, Kate Thornton and Kate Moss. There was also going to be a surprise appearance from the real Dennis Waterman, so I'd be lying if I said it didn't sound like a fun night. It was possibly going to be put out on DVD as well, and as I'm a huge fan of the show, and I love Matt and David's work, I was only too pleased to say yes. I was told that Matt wanted to run through the idea with me on the phone. Later that day, he called me up.

'First thanks for doing it,' said Matt.

'You're joking, it's a pleasure. Sounds like a right laugh.'

'Well, yeah, it will be,' said Matt. 'I just wanted to have this chat with you to make sure that you were cool with everything and that when it came to the night, you were a hundred per cent sure about what was happening.'

This sounded intriguing. 'Well, OK. I thought I was just going on stage with you.'

'You are,' replied Matt. 'Well, kind of with me. You're going to be part of the Fat Fighters sketch with Marjorie Dawes.'

For those of you who don't know, Marjorie is a horrible woman who hosts a slimming class. She abuses all her pupils and gives them grief about their weight. Sounded perfect for me.

'Marjorie will ask if there are any new members in the crowd and will then go and look for somebody for the weigh-in. I'll run into the audience and grab you on to the stage.'

So far so good.

'Then we'll have a little chat, and I'll make a few jokes, but do feel free to give me some back.'

Give him some back? How much abuse am I going to get?

'Then I'll pop you on the scales and say how much you weigh.'

'Which will be what?' I asked.

'Oh, about forty stone,' said Matt in his soft, calm voice. 'Then I'll have another go at you for being fat, and then bring on this huge Fat Fighters T-shirt for you to wear as a present, and it's massive, Chris, absolutely huge. So is all that OK with you?'

I thought about it for a millisecond. 'Matt, it sounds great. I'm up for it so I don't mind what you say.'

'Good,' said Matt. 'I just wanted to make sure because there'll be quite a few putdowns about your weight.'

It's not as if I haven't heard them all in real life anyway.

I asked for some tickets for friends but was told that as it was for charity, I would have to buy them, and they would be about £60 each. So not only was I going to get abused on stage, it was going to cost me money as well. Bloody Comic Relief, they're always after your cash!

I turned up on the night with Sophie and our friends Jodie and Abbie, and we found our seats. Comedy Dave was in the audience as well, along with a host of recognisable faces, including Thierry Henry, which made Sophie almost wet herself as she is a massive Arsenal fan. We ended up sitting next to Lenny Henry and Dawn French. It's fair to say that I'm not the smallest man in the world, and Lenny is huge and very broad, so the pair of us were crammed into our tiny theatre seats waiting for the show to start.

The lights went down and it began. All the characters from the show were there, and during almost every sketch somebody famous was involved. I was sitting near Jeremy Edwards who used to be in *Hollyoaks* and now does proper acting (!) and knew he was going on stage. What none of us knew was that David Walliams would tear down Jeremy's trousers, including his undercrackers. Jeremy fell to the floor and tried desperately to pull his pants back up, but it was too late. At least the first few rows got an eyeful!

The interval came and went, and then Marjorie Dawes walked out on to the stage and started the routine. Now I hadn't told my friends that I was going to be on, so when Matt started walking through the crowd towards us, everybody was smiling and laughing. Then Matt sees me and pulls me on to the stage, much to the amusement of my friends, and indeed Lenny Henry.

Once we were up there it was fine. Matt, or rather Marjorie, asked me what I did.

'I'm the Saviour of Radio 1,' I boasted.

'Radio? Oh I do telly. Never mind,' said Marjorie.

Then she talked about how fat I looked and then asked me to get on the scales.

'On you pop, sweetness and light. Well, sweetness at any rate.'

I stood on the scales and the indicator started whizzing round and round.

'Forty-three stone. Oh dear, it's not easy is it, Chris?' she said, as I just stood there and looked down in embarrassment – not real, of course. Remember, I am an actor too! If you want to see the rest of it, you'll have to buy the DVD and give some pennies to Comic Relief, but suffice to say, I was fat.

'You is FAT,' screamed Marjorie. 'You is so fat. You're the fatty bum bum of Radio 1.'

After the show we went upstairs for a drink and I met Kate Moss. I introduced myself to her, which I never normally do. She seemed nice and said that she liked the radio show, thought it was funny. That was a nice surprise, as I wouldn't have had Kate down for an early riser. Unless she's normally going to bed when I come on. Anyway, as with most school nights, we had to get home so I could have four hours' sleep before getting up the next morning. I bet you any money Kate wasn't listening then!

4

HOLIDAYS – FRIENDS INCLUSIVE

When I was a kid, we didn't have much. To quote Roy 'Chubby' Brown: 'We had fuck all. Remember a yo-yo? Well, we had a yo.'

It wasn't that we were poor, or at least I didn't feel like we were poor, but I certainly didn't feel rich. Don't get me wrong. I didn't live in the gutter or anything like that. I had my own bedroom and Kieron had his. Just because I'm writing a book, I'm not going to try and pretend that we were worse off than we really were. You always hear these so-called famous people who can't wait to tell you about how poor they were growing up. You see them on *Parkinson*, or *Oprah* if they're American, warbling on about how times were tough when they were younger and about how little money they had. Then they'll say something that gives it away, like: 'We could only afford two cars back in those days.' Or: 'When we went to Spain on holiday we all had to share the same room.' Went to Spain on holiday? We used to dream of going to Spain on holiday. Those tacky horrible-looking package holidays seemed like paradise to me when I was a kid. I remember my brother going to France on a school rugby trip. Now my brother and rugby went together like custard and chips. I swear he was only picked to go because he was a big lad and the school wanted kids who *looked* like rugby players. Anyway, off he went to France for a few days with the school. This to me was amazing. I'd had a few school trips myself but they weren't trips to France or anything like that. Mostly they were day trips. You know the kind of thing, you and all your classmates pile on to a local-company coach with your packed lunch and drive for three hours to some 'educational' place such as Beamish or an old Victorian museum. Fascinating.

I always remember my packed lunches would consist of some Heinz sandwich-spread sandwiches, a Munch Bunch yogurt, and maybe if I was lucky some arrowroot biscuits. Occasionally Mum would have a win at the Bingo and there might be a United chocolate biscuit thrown in too. Yummy!

However, once we all went to Hadrian's Wall in Northumberland AND we stayed overnight in a hotel. (When I say 'hotel', it seemed like a hotel at the time, but I think it was probably a hostel for cheap schools and dodgy kids.) The view from our window was on to the local fairground. We were told we could visit there as a treat before we left so we were all massively excited. We could see the roller-coaster from our room and got giddy at the thought of having a go on it. The excitement didn't last long, though. We looked out of the window in the afternoon and saw that the roller-coaster had stopped halfway up. Later on that night, as we were all going to bed, it was still stuck. 'Hey, lads, I'll be honest with ya, I don't think I'll be going on that bloody thing now,' I said. Instead of calling me a poof or a girl's blouse, ALL my mates in that little room looked back and nodded in agreement. We may have been kids but we weren't bloody daft!

The only other time I went away with my school was on a religious retreat. This was a very odd trip and to this day I can't see what the point of it was. It was to a place called Skipton, not that far from Leeds. We stayed in a huge religious house, which was something to do with priests or monks or nuns. I can't really remember because at the time I wasn't bothered. Bin Laden could've run the place for all I cared. All we were interested in was the fact that we were out of school and staying away from home. We had to go to mass and pray and stuff, but we did get some free time too. At the top of the building was a games room. This place was well cool. It had table tennis AND a pool table. I know that might not sound like much but when you're a kid, this is heaven. Also remember, I never had a pool table at home. I didn't have table tennis either. Like I said, we weren't poor, but we didn't have much, and what we did have was normally the cheaper version of the original.

Remember Connect 4? Yeah, well, we never had that. Instead we had a cheaper copy of it called 4-in-a-Row.

Remember ZX Spectrum and BBC computers? Well, we didn't have one of them either; we had a Texas Instruments computer. I'm not talking about a 'speak and spell' – this was a proper computer and you couldn't make it say rude words or anything like that.

Remember Simon, the colour electronic game where you had to remember the order of lights? Well, there was a copy of that game too, and guess which family had it.

On games day at school when you were allowed to bring in your favourite games from home, I would sit and play with EVERYBODY ELSE'S games. Downfall, Guess Who?, Battleships and even Electronic Battleships.

We did, however, have a Soda Stream. Now that made me feel like we'd won the Pools or Spot the Ball. For those of you who don't remember, Soda Streams were a clever contraption in which you'd stick some water and juice into a bottle, then shove the bottle into the Soda Stream machine and add the gas. Then you'd take the bottle out, shake it up and drink it. It was at this point that you'd realise it tasted like shit, but it didn't matter because you had made it yourself and that was cool. I was also lucky enough to have a Mister Softee set. This was the ice-lolly equivalent of a Soda Stream where you could make your own ice lollies and cups of flavoured crushed ice. That was wicked. Thanks, Mum and Dad.

So, because Mum and Dad spent all their money on cheap copies of kids' games and computers, it didn't leave much money to go on holiday. My dad worked as a postman for most of his life and did a hell of a lot of driving for the Post Office. There was hardly anywhere in the UK that Dad didn't know. Because of this we spent many holidays in some pretty parts of England, Scotland and Wales. The only time we ever crossed the sea, and I mean EVER, was to go to Ireland where Mum's from. It would be Dublin one summer, then Dublin the next summer and Dublin the summer after that. Sometimes Mum and Dad would treat us and we'd go to Dublin at Easter instead. Or we'd venture down to Tipperary, but it was always Ireland. I never minded this because I got to see all my Irish cousins and aunties and uncles, who I love very much, but I never went anywhere else abroad …

… until at the age of sixteen I got to go to America!! I had ALWAYS wanted to go to the States. I loved every single second I spent there. It was two weeks in Florida. One week in Orlando and the second week in St Petersburg. Sitting by a swimming pool was so weird to me but I absolutely loved it. I was also very lucky because my school mate Matthew Clarkson came with me and we had a right good time. As we were only sixteen we knew there was no chance of us getting a drink – you had to be twenty-one to get served alcohol there – so we just played in the pool and then at night hung out at the shopping malls. America fascinated me. Everybody spoke English yet it was so different from anything I was used to. I walked into a sports shop with Matthew one day and the fella who worked behind the counter looked at us and said, 'Hey, guys, what's up?'

Matthew and I looked at each other and then looked at the man.

'Nothing. We're only wanting to have a look round.'

We half expected to be kicked out. To be told that we weren't allowed in there without our parents.

On the last night of our first week, Matthew and I were messing around the hotel, not doing much but still having a laugh. We stuck our head into the bar where Dad was having a few beers. We sat down with him and were telling him what we'd been getting up to. Then the waitress came up and asked Dad if he wanted another beer.

'Yeah sure, another lager please, luv,' said Dad.

'Coming right up – and anything for you guys?' The waitress was looking at Matthew and me.

Now this was a difficult one. She was serving my dad a beer, and asking us if we wanted anything. Now we looked older than our sixteen years but I didn't think we looked twenty-one. However, we were sitting in a bar and she was asking us if we wanted a drink so maybe it was worth the risk. I looked at Dad and he simply looked back and smiled. I knew he was thinking the same thing as me, but of course he had nothing to worry about. He already had a beer coming, and besides, if we got turned down and the waitress laughed at us, he'd probably get a little kick out of it. I know I would. I decided I would go for it. I mean, maybe it's worth a shot. All I have to do is look confident, as if I'm not actually bothered about having a beer. After all she asked me, I didn't ask her.

'Erm, yeah, we'll have a couple of beers as well please, luv.'

I could feel the sweat on my forehead start to appear. Matthew, who hadn't said a word, was deafening in his silence as he sat there looking extremely guilty.

'Three beers coming right up.'

JESUS CHRIST, I DON'T BELIEVE IT. RESULT!

'There you go,' said Dad.

'Is that all right?' I asked, seeking Dad's approval.

'Yeah, why not, just don't be silly.'

'We won't, Mr Moyles, thank you,' said Matthew.

The second week of the holiday was pretty much swimming-pool-based. Matthew and I had befriended some lads from Wakefield who were a couple of years older than us, and we spent a lot of time with them. One night they decided to try and get some beers themselves, so Matthew and I tagged along. Understandable, as we were now the under-age-drinking Kings of America.

We walked into a bar in the hotel. A spit-and-sawdust place that wasn't anything special. If we could get a drink in the last hotel, then this place should be a piece of piss.

'How do, luv, you alreet?' said our spokesperson.

'Hold your horses, guys. If you fellas wanna have some beers then I'm gonna need to see some ID. You need to be twenty-one so I'm going to have to see some of your passports.'

SHITE.

'What, even mine?' said the biggest bloke in our group.

'No, not yours, darlin', you're OK. But I will need to see yours, and yours.'

This was like being in some kind of prisoner-of-war camp. This over-weight American woman (hope I'm not stating the obvious here!) was like the most important woman in the world.

'I'm also gonna need to see yours, darlin'.'

A night of beer rested on her say-so. She went through the entire group of us, pointing to each one and deciding whether or not we had to produce ID in order to get some alcohol.

'You're all right, honey, but not your friend.'

I knew what my chances were, and I was ready to leave the bar with my head held low. Eventually it was my turn.

'You're fine, sweetheart ...'

JESUS CHRIST, I DON'T BELIEVE IT. RESULT AGAIN!

Now I was pleased that I was allowed yet another beer in another bar, but seriously, did I really look twenty-one? I was sixteen for Christ's sake. Thanks for the beer but this was starting to hurt my feelings.

It was another two years before I ventured abroad again. Obviously, after Florida there were more trips to Ireland, but then when I was eighteen, I landed a job at Radio Luxembourg, in Luxembourg. This was a strange yet beautiful place. Amazingly picturesque and breath-taking in its scenery. I lived in a place called Limpertsberg, which was virtually in the centre of the city. For the next nine months it became my home and I eventually got used to it. In fact, just about the same time I got used to it, we were told that Radio Luxembourg was to close down and we were all out of a job. So I had no choice but to pack my things and head back home, still only eighteen years old.

On my nineteenth birthday I was back at home with Mum and Dad in Leeds and working in Bradford. Amazingly, it would be another four years before I went overseas again. Obviously not including Ireland. I can't keep explaining that. I ALWAYS went there, so please take it for granted – even though I may not mention I went there, I did.

I had longed to go back to America. Something about that place appealed to me. Exactly what, I wasn't sure. America is a bloody big place and I had only been to two different bits of it, and both of those were in Florida. I was desperate to get out and discover more of this amazing land, and I knew exactly where my next stop would be.

LOS ANGELES, CALIFORNIA.

I'd always wanted to go there, and six months after I started working for Radio 1, I booked my ticket and was all set. At the time I was going out with a girl called Helen, so actually I booked two tickets, but now I'm just being picky.

After what seemed like months, but was only a few weeks, the big day arrived and we headed off to Heathrow. We checked in, cleared security and did some last-minute shopping. For what, I have no idea. My girlfriend Sophie even now always wants to go shopping at the airport. Is this a woman thing? I don't think there's anything I ever need to buy at an airport, except maybe an adapter plug or a book. Every time we go away I am amazed at the amount of shops there are at the airport.

Do I want a new handbag? No.

Do I fancy buying myself three white shirts? No, I've packed already, thank you.

Oh look, a car! What the fuck are those doing there, and do you actually know anybody who has ever won a car while killing time at the airport? And if you do win it, what do you do with it? Are you allowed to keep it parked up in the middle of Terminal 4 while you enjoy your ten days in the sun?

'Congratulations, Mr Moyles, you have won this fabulous Ferrari!'

'Wow, I don't believe it. Thank you so much.'

'My pleasure, sir. Now just be careful driving it through security, the gate is a little bit tight.'

'Oh right, well, actually I'm heading off on holiday for a week so I was wondering if I could keep it here, or maybe you could deliver it to my house when I return home.'

'No, sir. Either take it with you now or I will keep it!'

My mobile rang and it was my friend Mitch Johnson, voiceover man and one of the funniest and nicest people I know. Back then, however, he was also very unpredictable, but in a funny way.

'Let's go the pub!' shouted Mitch.

'Are you mental? I'm at Heathrow,' I said.

'Oh wow. Where are you going?'

'LA, remember. I've only been telling you for the last month that I'm going. Do you not remember?'

'Oh yeah, LA. How cool. Oh, what a shame. I've got the rest of the day off and I thought we could spend it in the pub.'

'Well, sorry to disappoint you, Mitch, but I'm not giving up LA to sit in our local boozer. You'll have to come to LA instead if you fancy a pint,' I said.

'Ha ha. What a great idea, I'll see you there. Bye bye bye bye bye bye.'

He always ends his phone conversations by repeating the word 'bye' until he puts the phone down. As I said, he's a funny man.

Anyway the time came for us to get on the plane. I was so excited I could hardly speak. These days I'm scared of flying so I don't say much when I get on a plane anyway, apart from, 'Can you avoid turbulence please and make sure the captain doesn't fall asleep when we're coming in to land?'

(Here's something I've always wondered about. You know occasionally when you're about to land and the plane suddenly and without any explanation pulls back up and you have to circle round and land again? Is that the captain having an unexpected sneezing fit and accidentally pulling back on the wheel? Just a thought.)

So Helen and I are sitting on the plane just about to taxi to the runway, when some idiot's phone starts to ring. I hate those people. Don't they realise that the ringing could interfere with the plane and kill us all?

Are these people stupid?

I mean it's ridiculous.

It's selfish.

SHIT. IT'S MY PHONE!

'Hello,' I whisper.

'Hello, it's Mitch again. Whereabouts in LA are you staying?'

One of the cabin crew approached me, and she didn't look happy.

'Please, sir, switch your phone off right now.'

'Yeah, I'm sorry about that.'

'What? Where are you staying?'

'What? Oh, the Beverly Hills Hilton.'

'Sir. You have to switch your phone off now, please.'

'OK, see you for a pint,' said Mitch.

'OK, I'm sorry. I'm switching it off now.'

'OK, bye,' said Mitch.

'Mitch?'

'Sir?'

'What?'

'*TURN YOUR PHONE OFF.*'

'All right, it's off, keep your knickers on. Oh I forgot, you're cabin crew, you're probably not wearing any.'

She started to walk away. She wasn't amused.

'It was only a joke.'

We landed at night-time and it was raining. I hired a car and was amazed that they simply hand you the keys. That's it. I'd never driven before in America, let alone Los Angeles in the pouring rain at night. I shat myself for about an hour until we eventually reached the hotel. Now I booked the Beverly Hills Hilton without even looking at a picture of it because I thought it sounded very grand and elegant. For legal reasons all I will say now is that I always check what the hotel looks like before I travel. We found our room and it was a smoking room. I could tell that from the brown-stained walls and smell of stale smoke. It was hardly glamorous. Helen and I had a couple of drinks before crashing out.

The next morning we got up and were about to go for breakfast when I noticed that our phone had a little flashing red light on it.

'Did you hear the phone ring in the night?' I asked Helen.

'Not that I was aware of, no.'

I pressed the red light and was told by an American computer lady that I had a voicemail message waiting for me, and guess what the message said.

'Hello good morning. It's Mitch here. What a strange hotel this is, although my room is very nice. I have a view of the Hollywood sign. That's quite groovy. Anyway give me a ring when you wake up and we'll go out for a drive. I'm in 711, just like the shop. Bye bye bye bye bye bye.' Clunk.

I put down the receiver and just stared at the phone.

'Who was that?' asked Helen.

'Well,' I said nervously, 'that was Mitch. Apparently he's in room 711, just like the shop.'

'WHAT? Tell me you're joking. He'd better not be in the same hotel. We've only just got here.' I don't think Helen was looking forward to spending a week in LA with her boyfriend and her boyfriend's crazy mate.

'Don't worry, he'll be messing about. I'll call his room.'

I dialled 711, just like the shop, and waited.

There was no answer.

'See. I told you he's not here. He's just messing around.'

Now don't get me wrong. I LOVE my friend Mitch, and if I'm honest I was secretly hoping that he had flown out to LA for a drink. That would've been very cool. However, I understood Helen's point. It was our first time away together and I'm sure most women wouldn't want to be away with their fella plus his mate from the local pub. Besides, he must have work to do or—

RING RING!

The phone in the room began to ring, hence the 'ring ring' that I just wrote there. Helen looked at me. I looked at her, and I picked the phone up.

'Hello?'

'Hey, it's Mitchy Mitch here. What a beautiful day it is. I hired a car, so let's go for a drive through LA!'

'There is no way whatsoever that you are here in this hotel,' I said, secretly wishing he were.

'Of course I'm here. I'm in room 711.'

'Yeah yeah, I know, just like the shop,' I replied. 'If you're really here in the hotel, then come and knock on our door and we'll go for breakfast.'

'Oh good idea. I'm starving,' said Mitch.

I put the phone down. Helen was still looking at me.

'Look, he's not gonna get on a plane and fly halfway around the world for a pint, Helen. This is a man who lives approximately two minutes' walk from the pub, and when you arrange to meet him Monday evening at six, he turns up Tuesday evening at eight. Yet you honestly think he's come all the way to the west coast of America because I told him to? Come on, don't be daft. He's messing around. He'll call back in a few minutes and laugh at us for even thinking that he—'

DING DONG!

The doorbell for the room rang, hence the 'ding dong' that I just wrote there. I opened the door.

'Told you!' said Mitch, as he walked straight past me and into the room. 'Hello, Helen. Oh wow, look at your room. It's bigger than mine, but I have a really nice view of the Hollywood sign. Now are you ready, because I've hired a car and we can go for a drive.'

'MITCH, WHAT THE HELL ARE YOU DOING IN LA?' I screamed.

Mitch's happy face fell and he looked confused. 'You said come out and we'll have a drink. So I checked my diary, didn't have any work till Thursday, so here I am. Right, are you ready?'

And with that, the three of us jumped in his car and went for breakfast.

I LOVE MITCH.

PAUL MCKENNA ON MOYLES

I have known Chris for years. I believe he is very talented and has a truly original style when so many DJs these days sound the same. However, a couple of years ago I was having a party. It was a last-minute decision and so rather than send out invitations I decided to call everyone. Chris never answers his phone so I left a message. Now I only ever see him with his posse so I assumed he might want to bring them with him to feel more comfortable. So, as well as inviting him, I said, 'And if you want to bring some friends, that will be fine.'

Next thing I hear he has been playing my message on the air and analysing what I mean by 'bring some friends'. It's not bad enough that everyone now thinks I am having some kind of swingers' orgy, but all the people I know and haven't invited are on the phone saying they've heard about the party and they're going to see me on Friday. So I had a house rammed with people and the bastard never even showed up himself!

5

RADIO vs TELEVISION

By now you should be aware that I've always wanted to be on the radio. I can't help it, I'm a radio guy, I just love the medium. It's simple, quick, easy and incredibly powerful. You can be lying in bed or driving your car. You can be sitting on a bus or a train or lying out in the sun in your back garden. Radio can get everywhere television can't and for that reason I will ALWAYS prefer radio to TV.

However, television is deemed to be king, despite have appeared a long time after radio. When the wireless first appeared on the scene, it was adored by the masses. The whole family would gather in the living room to sit and listen to their favourite programmes. Then this new invention came along that was like radio but had moving pictures. My dad remembers when the first TV arrived in his street. Forget the family, it was now all the neighbours gathered together, staring at this magical, massive box that took up a whole corner of the room. It was exciting and new, and because people could see who was talking, everybody wanted to witness this thing called 'television'. And I suppose it's still like that today. Sure radio is popular, indeed the listening figures for radio in general are growing,

Now <u>this</u> is fashion.

Get out of the way you crazy squares. I'm on a tricycle!

Young and fit.

Old and fat!

What's worse? The hair or the short trousers?

Embarrassingly, this was taken in June.

Carol Vorderman
is on the left.

Radio legend Simon Bates is on the right.

No comment.

On the Friday Night Project.
Again, no comment.

Effing cooking with effing Gordon.

Gordon, Sophie and me.

but it seems to be television that everybody talks about. I'd like to think that I'm changing that, turning conversations from:

'Did you see that thing on Big Brother *last night?'*

To:

'Did you hear what Chris Moyles was doing this morning?'

I know that sounds a bit big-headed but it's what I do. I want everybody to listen to the radio show and talk about it in the same way they would talk about a TV show. I also want to get as many listeners as I can, and appearing on TV is one way to achieve that and spread the message. So since I started at Radio 1, I have done more and more bits on the telly. I prefer radio but I understand that it helps to appear on TV. And, of course, I like appearing on TV. But which is best? Is television better than radio? Well, here are some good and bad points about TV.

GOOD about TV: **THE POWER**

Being on the radio five days a week is very powerful, but there's something to be said for actually being in people's living rooms in the evening and staring right into their eyes. People are used to me being on the radio, but even after my ten years at Radio 1, friends get excited when they see my fat face on the box.

BAD about TV: **TIME AND MONEY**

If during the radio show we want Dominic to be stood outside the Eiffel Tower – not that I can imagine a reason why we would want to – we simply stick some street noises on, the theme to *'Allo 'Allo* and get Dom to speak in a rubbish French accent. Voila, we are in Paris. If you want to do the same thing on TV, you need to go there, or build an elaborate set. Either way, it costs time and money. Radio is theatre of the mind. You have to imagine what the studio looks like, or visualise Dom in the cold morning air of France. You don't have to see with your eyes; you 'see' it in your head.

GOOD about TV: IT PAYS WELL

You think that radio pays well – it's nothing compared to television. Because it costs more to make, there's more money in it. Sure, you might have to hang around all day waiting, but you get well paid for it. I've earned for one TV show what I get in a month for the radio show.

BAD about TV: IT'S SO BLOODY SLOW

You turn up and you go through the script. TV needs a script because everybody needs to know what is happening now and what is happening next. Then you walk through the show and have a little practice to check everything is OK. Then you get dressed and have a rehearsal to ensure that everything that's OK looks good on camera. And then you do the actual show. With radio, you turn up and you do it, then you get everything ready for the next day. Easy.

GOOD about TV: IT CAN BE REALLY EXCITING

Being in the radio studio every day is still really cool. But being on a TV set with all the lights and the cameras is great. Stick an audience in there and you get an immediate reaction to jokes. It's brilliant when you do a gag and you can see the people in front of you laughing.

BAD about TV: LIVE RADIO IS MORE EXCITING

So there, radio wins!

Besides, who wants to be on television anyway? That used to be a valid question. In the current climate of reality TV, it seems that the question should now be: Who doesn't want to be on television? Any wannabe from any walk of life can now ease their way on to our screens in any manner of shows. It also seems to me that the thicker you are, the better your chances. Seriously? You know that the more stupid and vacuous the person, the more likely they'll end up on *Big Brother*. If you're so dumb that you don't realise you can't sing a note and that in fact you are as good a singer as Stevie Wonder is a forensic scientist, then your fifteen minutes await you on a singing contest. If you're reading this and you're a backward simpleton who doesn't know jack shit, then good news: you could be a reality TV star. Oh, how proud your parents will be.

I've done a few things on TV since getting into radio. Some of these have been brilliant and some have been absolute pants. Millions have seen some appearances and others have barely been seen at all.

My first crack at TV presenting was when my family took us to the holiday camp Pontins. Mum hated every second of it as it was a little bit common for her tastes, but I loved it cos they had their own radio and TV channel. I banged on the door and asked for a look round and they just stuck me on camera. That was cool and it also helped give me something to do for the rest of the week. There are only so many times you can kick the crocodile mascot up the arse and then run off. After this I stayed away from TV for a good few years. This was mainly because I had school as I was only about thirteen.

I became reunited with TV when I first arrived at Radio 1 and was asked to be a record reviewer for a show on Sky. I didn't even have Sky at the time, but who cared? I was going to be on television. The show was called *Showbiz Weekly* and it was recorded in the trendy Met Bar in London. All I had to do was talk about the new releases that week and occasionally interview some pop stars. Easy enough, I thought. The only downside was the presenter. Tania Bryer was a former weather girl who had risen to the dizzy heights of Sky TV. I was amazed at how she was treated by the production crew. They would bend over backwards for the woman, who in my opinion wasn't even that good. She was quite posh and I'm not sure how many of the records and bands I talked about she had heard of or was even interested in.

I did that for a while and then in 1998 Dave and I were asked if we wanted to be part of a new music channel called UK Play. All they wanted was the pair of us stood in front of a screen introducing videos, but we wanted more. So eventually *The Chris Moyles Show* was created. Well, we had a set at least, which consisted of a door, a desk for me, a piano for Dave to sit at despite the fact he can't play the piano, and a TV screen behind me disguised as a window for us to use in hilarious comedy sketches. There was no money in it, and it was rubbish. Actually, I'll take that back: it wasn't rubbish, it was very hit and miss, with the emphasis on miss. However, there were a few funny gags on the show where we would edit ourselves into music videos or film silly sketches out on the street. My favourite was when I introduced a new item into the show.

'Here you are, Dave, it's our new feature, "Dave Shags Supermodels".'

'Hey, I like the sound of that,' said Dave with a huge cheeky smile on his face.

We then ran a video of a geeky bloke saying: 'Hello, I'm Dave Shag, and these are my supermodels. This week, Claudia Schiffer.'

You get it? It was Dave Shag's not Dave Shags, you see. Oh how we laughed.

Surprisingly, Dave and I did three series of the show, totalling over 150 programmes for the channel. Don't bother searching for them on the internet; you'll only be disappointed.

My next big break in TV was a show that EVERYBODY has forgotten about. I was asked to be a team captain on a brand new ITV comedy panel show called *Casting Couch*.

Now I have finally made it, I remember thinking. Once again, I was very wrong.

The show went out on a Monday night at about 10.30pm and was hosted by double act Mel and Sue. I played team captain along with Tamara Beckwith. Yes, that's right, the former It Girl. Before I met her I was expecting her to be a nightmare, but surprisingly she was very nice. I even got a Christmas card from her, which I thought was sweet. I didn't send her one back and I haven't heard from her since. I must point out that I don't think these two incidents are related, unless she is really fucking precious about Christmas cards! Anyway, each week we were joined by a whole host of big names and not-so-big names. It was the usual comedy panel show with questions about celebrities and entertainment stories of the week. And once again, it didn't do very well. It was cancelled after just one series.

After that it was the odd little show here and there and occasionally an audition for something. I remember sneaking into *The Big*

Breakfast house early one Saturday morning to record a secret pilot show. Nobody knew we were doing it and we even had to sign in under pseudonyms. All a bit silly really, but it was quite good fun. Then in the summer of 2002, it all changed when Chris Evans asked me if I thought he and I should do a show together. I foolishly said yes! Now I have talked about this situation a couple of times before, but for you, the reader, and for one more read only, I will talk about it for the last time.

I had met Chris a few times before but it was after a chance meeting in LA (how tossy does that sound?) that we got talking about a TV show. On my return to London I was asked if I wanted to meet up with him and talk about an idea he had. He came round to my flat and we chatted for a while about the show and he said we could probably get it commissioned by Channel 5. And he was right. A few weeks later we walked into a meeting at the station's head office in London, and half an hour later walked out with a new TV series.

> 'So let me get this straight. We have just convinced them to give us a series, and we haven't even got an office, a location or any staff yet? What the hell do we do now?'
>
> Chris smiled at me and said, 'Let's go get a drink and make a list of people to hire!'

I must admit it was all very exciting. We found a quiet bar and came up with the names of some people we had both worked with before.

Once the team was in place, we all headed down to Chris's huge country home for our first meeting. Now I knew that Chris was unpredictable, to say the least, so I was prepared for anything, or so I thought. I was, if I'm honest, flattered by his enthusiasm for the show and for me. Then he did a little speech to the new team that blew me away. Chris had recently come back from a spell of living in the States. He told us that the one thing he had learnt there was that 'talent was king'. And how the show would succeed if everybody backed me up.

> 'We all take a bullet for Chris. That's how it works and that's
> how the show will be a success.'

Jesus Christ, that was nice to hear. Normally people want to put a bullet in me, not take one for me.

We decided the show would be live from a pub with a small audience. Now, I could go on and try and make it sound like some ground-breaking moment of British television, but basically it was a cheap version of *TFI Friday*. 'It's *TFI* without the budget,' I said in countless interviews before the show even aired. We found a pub in North London and began to do some pilot shows to practise. It was to be called *Chris Moyles Live*, which suited me. A week before we went on air, they decided to change the name to *Live With Chris Moyles*.

> 'This is bad news. It's a sign you know,' I moaned to Sophie
> and my friend Jon Culshaw one evening.

> 'A sign of what?' they asked.

> 'Well, *Chris Moyles Live* is my name and the word "Live", right?
> If they change the name of the show to *Live With Chris Moyles*,
> that means that if they're not happy with me, they change me.
> Then they change the "Chris Moyles" bit to somebody else's
> name. *Live With Dermot O'Leary* or *Live With Keith Chegwin*.
> It's like they're hedging their bets before we've even done the

first show, and I'll be honest, it doesn't fill me with confidence,' I whinged.

'Oh stop being paranoid,' said Sophie. 'Think about the bullet that he's going to take for you.'

The first show went well, with the exception of a moment of bad language from one of the callers. There had been a slight earthquake in Birmingham over the weekend, so I asked if he had felt the quake.

'I fucking did yeah!' came the reply.

Thanks so much, sir, for your contribution.

After the first show, Finlo Rohrer from BBC News Online, wrote:

> *It is often said funny, live television is near impossible to pull off, but Moyles does not give himself a head start with a train of bad games and tepid jokes that would be more at home at an irritating freshers' night than on primetime television.*

> *For Moyles, it seems like the transition to television has caught him out.*

And this was after the first show, for fuck's sake. I know a lot of people hate my guts and can't wait to see me fail, but Jesus at least give it a week before you say it's shit. Ian Hyland in the *Sunday Mirror* did. After the first five shows he wrote:

> *On the trailers for* Live With Chris Moyles *our roly-poly hero tried to sum it up in five words. Having watched it I can now do likewise: I Give It Two Months.*

Well, that just shows you what an idiot Ian Hyland is. It lasted three months!

The show aired live every weekday evening at seven, and my confidence was building with each show. The only problem was that the format was getting changed all the time. We'd just about find our feet with the order of items and then they'd get changed or dropped. Bits I could play with and have some fun with got shortened so much there was hardly any time for me to have a proper laugh. But everybody seemed happy enough and Channel 5 even commissioned it for another series when we were not even halfway through the run.

Then one night we did a show that I thought was a bit poor. I must explain that I judged the show by my standards, and on that night I thought I was like a presenter puppet going through the motions of a show. I couldn't play with items as there wasn't enough time, or there was too much time on an item I wasn't as interested in. I was obviously disappointed after the show. I went upstairs to the cupboard where I got changed and Chris knocked on the door and came in. He asked what was wrong.

> 'I thought it was rubbish tonight. As in I thought I was rubbish. There's just no room for me to breathe. I get an item that I wanna play with and get some nice laughs out of but there's not time for me to do it.'

'It was fine tonight, don't worry,' said Evans.

'But fine isn't enough. We've crammed the show so tightly with features that there's no room for me to make them funny in my own way. Anybody could have presented that show tonight, and I thought the idea was for me to make it my own.'

I went on explaining that we should do less in the show instead of more. Chris stayed silent all the way through my rant and I knew he was a bit pissed off. I thought he might have agreed with me and been a bit annoyed with himself for letting it happen.

WRONG.

We ended the chat with me telling him that we had to have confidence in me to pull these items off and to have fewer things to do and more time to make them funny. By the time he left, I had cheered myself up and knew that the next night's show would be a great one.

Chris didn't turn up for the show the next night. He didn't turn up the night after that either. In fact, he didn't turn up at all before the end of the series at Christmas!

Whoops!

He did turn up at my local pub one Sunday, though. A mutual friend called me and asked why I wasn't in the pub with everybody.

'Who's everybody?' I asked.

'Everybody from your TV show, mate. We're all in the boozer at the end of your road. Chris is here as well.'

Now I'm no Magnum PI but I thought that maybe Chris was avoiding me. Well, I hadn't seen him for weeks and I was still slightly emotional from his 'We all take a bullet for Chris' speech, so I was curious as to why he had abandoned me and the show. I got to the pub and was welcomed by all who saw me, with one exception. Just to make sure I wasn't being paranoid, I made my way over to where Chris was. Remember, at this time I was presenting a TV show that he was producing, despite not having turned up to the show for weeks. I sat down at the table and the moment my arse touched the seat, Evans stood up and walked over to talk to somebody else. Not a good start, I thought. It was definitely a blank. But I thought I would double-check. I decided I should buy everybody a drink: that way I would have to ask everybody individually what he or she wanted, and he would have to speak to me. I went round the group, and when I got to Chris I asked:

'You having a drink, pal?'

'Guinness,' said Evans, not even looking at me.

I went to the bar, bought the drinks (it was a fucking expensive double-check) and began handing them out one by one. I handed Chris the Guinness and he took it and muttered 'Cheers' before walking over to somebody else. That was definitely a blank. So two blanks, I thought. I might as well go for the hat trick. One of the people sitting at the table with Chris called me over. Once again, as I sat down, Evans stood up. This was now so farcical it made me laugh. Here was a grown man, my fucking boss, trying to avoid having any contact with me whatsoever. It was at this point that I thought I might not be coming back to host the second series.

After the last show, we all had a party. I made a point of shaking hands, thanking everybody for all their hard work. Everybody except for Chris Evans, who by the time I left hadn't even shown up.

On a lighter note, it was Christmas, and Sophie and I headed off on our first-ever holiday together. I splashed out with my TV money and bought two tickets on Concorde to New York. I'm so pleased I did that. We then flew to Barbados for five days in the sun. While I was there I got a message to call my agent back in London.

'I've just had a press release faxed through to the office. It says that Christian O'Connell is the new host of *Live With* and that you are no longer hosting the show. Instead you're working on other projects with Channel 5.'

What a surprise. I hate it when my paranoia is correct. Oh well: it paid for a new patio and a holiday in New York so I suppose it wasn't all that bad.

Now as I write I have been doing more television and it seems to be working a lot better than *Live With*. I recently presented an episode of *The Friday Night Project* on Channel 4. That was really fun. As I was saying earlier, television takes time, so it was a long day but it was very enjoyable. Also Alan Carr and Justin Lee Collins were both funny and supportive of me so it felt a lot easier.

I'll probably do more TV but I want to make sure it's the right show for me. I'm sick of critics saying I look uncomfortable on TV or I don't seem myself. Fuck off. It's always going to be different to the radio show – you can see my face for a start. Also, because I'm quite a heavy boy, I often look like a sack of potatoes in ill-fitting clothes. But if I get myself a stylist and lose some weight, who knows, maybe I could be the next Davina McCall!

6

TREADMILLS ARE NOT JUST FOR CLOTHES

For as long as I can remember, I have been a little tubby. I was a little tubby at school. I was a bigger little tubby when I started work. Over the years I have mastered the art of being a tubby. Even when I lost a load of weight, I was still fat. It's a fact of life and I'm used to it now. It amuses me when somebody makes 'fat' jokes, as if I didn't know I was overweight and will be shocked and appalled by such nasty and hurtful information. I look in the mirror daily and see a chubby fella looking back at me, so it is no longer a surprise, and merely reveals the purveyor of such insults as having a poor comedic eye.

Occasionally I do something about my weight. I have starved myself of booze for a month. Some people call it 'staying off the beer' but I like to call it 'Beer Starvation', as that's what it feels like. I'm telling you, Terry Waite chained to a radiator for weeks on end sounds like a dream to me, compared with having to watch a football game in the pub while drinking orange juice. (OK, maybe a bad example.)

I have also drifted in and out of a regular training programme. This training usually consists of some walking home from work, and some actual running. But more accurately, my 'training' consists of boring all my friends by telling them what I'm GOING to do to lose weight, rather than actually doing it. (Talking lots can burn calories too you know.)

I even joined a gym a few years back. When I switched from working in the afternoons to doing the breakfast show, I thought: *Great. I can work till midday, then go straight to the gym for a couple of hours and still have time in the afternoon to chill out.*

Over a year went by and I had indeed lost loads of pounds. £50 a month to be precise, and I never went more than five times. Shocking.

I did once lose quite a lot of weight and got myself into fairly decent shape. I met an amazing woman called Jane. This woman was fit. Not just in the looks department, which she was if you like fit-looking women with bigger arm muscles than you. I mean she was physically fit. She could run up the stairs and not be out of breath by the time she got to the top. (To this day I'm impressed by people who don't get out of breath after bending down to tie their shoelaces!) Jane worked with the team and me when we did the afternoon show in 2000. With the catchy title of 'Gym Lady Jane', she set about putting together a training schedule for each member of the team. And what a team it was.

First, our producer, Will 'Grey Ed' Kinder. Now, at this time of his life Will enjoyed a cigarette. Most mornings he and I would have time for a quick fag before going for a run. This usually appalled Jane, but we thought it was natural to smoke before a run. You'd be too tired afterwards.

Then there was Lizzie. A very cute tomboy of a girl who was tiny in height and in body mass. This girl didn't need to lose ANY weight at all. She didn't need a bloody good personal trainer. What Lizzie needed was a bloody good burger. Lizzie, like the rest of us, liked a drink. Gin and slim to be precise. However, she did put her heart into the training and did very well.

Add to this list of fine athletes my one and only radio wife, Comedy Dave. It's fair to say that Dave is quite competitive. However, he also gets bored easily, which doesn't make for the best training partner. A typical training session would see Dave burn off running at top speed, get tired, bored and then stop.

Finally, there was me. Overweight, smelling of fags, and in running shirt and shorts looking like an elephant wrapped in clingfilm. Strangely, I seemed to Jane to be the biggest challenge. No shit? However, I was determined to make it work. I dived straight into my brand new training regime.

In the early days Jane went easy on us. We'd meet in Regent's Park, stretch out and warm up, and then go for a run. At first we were to run for only six minutes. Six?? I could do that in my sleep. Actually, no, I couldn't. After six minutes of running, ALL of us were knackered. How pathetic. But we did it, and felt very pleased with ourselves for running for slightly longer than the time it takes to boil a kettle.

As the weeks went by, the runs got longer.

Six minutes became ten minutes.

Ten minutes became fifteen minutes.

And fifteen minutes became over twenty.

Oh, the joy of running for twenty minutes! Not in the running itself, mind you. During a run, if we were particularly tired, Jane would say how good we were going to feel when we finished. Of course we would. Kick me in the balls for half an hour and I feel better when you finish!

After a year we all got weighed for the show. Amazingly, I had lost two stone. I was delighted. Not just because of the weight loss but also because I was a lot fitter than I'd ever been. I didn't get short of breath so easily. I could even get out of bed without needing oxygen.

I was proud of myself, and so was Jane. So proud that she decided to enter me for the World's Biggest Half-Marathon, The Great North Run. Cheers!

Training for this thirteen-mile run was not fun. I never understand people who say they enjoy running. It's rubbish. I'll admit I LOVE the feeling when it's over but I HATE the feeling of actually running. Jane did her best to encourage me by telling me that if I didn't train I wouldn't finish the course and I'd look stupid in front of everybody. So for four days a week we'd meet up and go for a nice long run. Yippee. One day Jane even managed to organise Paula Radcliffe to train with us. That was a stupid idea. We went for a twenty-minute run with her and by the end of it none of us had the energy to even to speak.

Eventually the time came and we headed up to Newcastle to take part in a hellish, horrible half-marathon.

Now, being semi-famous, I was placed with all the other semi-famous people who were running that year. There was:

Frank Bruno, the boxer and pantomime dame.

Gordon Ramsay, a chef or something. (It was 2001 – the only chefs I had heard of were Rusty Lee and Delia Smith.)

Sir Jimmy Savile OBE (which I believe stands for 'One Boiled Egg').

Ray Stubbs, the BBC football presenter.

Former footballer now football commentator and pundit Mark Bright, who put his number in my phone as 'The Prince of Stoke'. What an accolade.

Lots of people from Emmerdale Farm.

And finally the legend that was John 'Motty' Motson.

We took our positions at the front and waited for the gun to start us off.

I could write a detailed account of every mile of that horrible run, but I can't be arsed. Suffice to say it was as enjoyable as sitting in a dentist's chair for an entire day. Here is the 13-mile race, shortened version:

The Great North Run has a bloody long hill in it that goes on forever.

Frank Bruno passed me about half a mile into the run.

I passed Jimmy Savile about three miles into the run.

One of the men from *Emmerdale* stopped to have a pee at the side of the road.

The 'oggy oggy oggy' chants from fellow runners that were so loud at the beginning of the race slowly died down each passing mile, until about eight miles in they suddenly stopped.

The 'pacer' they give you to run with disappeared at about four miles in and I never saw 'em again.

Despite having passed Jimmy Savile miles earlier, when I crossed the finishing line I spotted him in the VIP section all wrapped up enjoying a nice post-run beverage. I couldn't spot a bead of sweat on him! (I swear I NEVER fucking saw him pass me – but I suppose I might have been busy gasping for breath at the time).

Being in sight of the finishing line is the best feeling ever.

Jane ran with me all the way and if it weren't for her I would never have finished. Halfway through the course she told me: 'Chris, you may as well slow down and take it easy as you're not going to finish in under two hours.'

This was our magic time limit. If I'd been able to finish the race in less than two hours we would both have been delighted.

'I don't want you getting cramp and pulling out cos you're trying to beat a time that you'll never reach,' she explained.

Bless Gym Lady Jane. Not only was she a great trainer, she was also a very convincing liar. As we approached the finishing line, I looked up to see that the clock read 1hr 56m 23s.

'Shit, look at the time!' I screamed.

'I know. Sorry I said that earlier, but you were running so quick I was genuinely worried that you *would* get cramp and not finish.

This is the quickest you've ever run and you will finish in under two hours.'

I was delighted. I found a secret supply of energy and burst through the other runners towards the finishing line. My time was a respectable 1 hour and 57 minutes, and I was knackered.

I'd done it. I had run a half-marathon in under two hours and was now sweating like a good 'un, chatting away with Gordon Ramsay and Ray Stubbs about how great our times were. Gordon, of course, completed the run in about half an hour, the flash bastard.

Then we all got up and waited for the coach to take us back to our hotel. I felt great, and very proud of myself. It was quite an emotional experience for me because this was also to be the last run that Gym Lady Jane and I did together. She was leaving Britain to go abroad and look after a ladies' netball team or something. So it was nice that we ended our story on a high.

At about this time, I started presenting *Live With Chris Moyles*, which, as you know (cos I've told you, not cos anybody watched it!), was in the setting of a real live pub. I had trained for almost two years with Jane. I had lost three and a half stone and had finished the World's Biggest Half-Marathon in less than two hours. Jane left, I started working in a pub every night, and by Christmas, just over three months later, I hadn't run a mile and was a stone heavier.

In the New Year I tried again but it was too late. My former friend, the evil lord lager, had returned to my life and drowned my desire to run. Within eighteen months I was back to the weight I was when I met Jane. My training days were well and truly over. My beer belly returned and I could no longer see my feet. Maybe 'being fat' was my thing.

Then one day, out of the blue, I got asked if I'd like a treadmill. Regular listeners to the show will know that on occasion we get sent free stuff. CDs, obviously, but also clothes, trainers, beer, tickets for shows, that kind of thing. However, I have never been offered a treadmill before, and I was very excited.

I had never really been THAT upset by my weight. I think deep down I thought that one day I'd lose the flab and get fit. And then I had done exactly that, and spectacularly blown it and put all the weight back on. I had tried running again but could never last longer than a week. (That's not non-stop running for a week, you understand. I'm not Forrest bloody Gump!) Try as I might, I couldn't get back to my old training regime with Jane. I'd get up off the couch, put my running stuff on and head outside into the cold streets of London, where awaiting paparazzi, hoping to get a money shot of Oscar-winning Gwyneth Paltrow with her children, would be quite happy to settle for a fat DJ running down the street sweating like a pig on a barbecue.

Nah, what I needed was a treadmill …

I had always mocked people who bought running machines for their homes. My friend Darryl used his as a large and elaborate clothes horse. I was determined not to go the same way. So I vowed to myself that when it turned up, I would use it. And I mean USE IT, and not just to hang clothes off.

Just before Christmas 2006, the guys arrived at my place with the biggest treadmill you have ever seen. It had a TV on it, for Christ's sake. It was amazing. And it was also too large to fit through the front door of the flat, so it had to be sent back. Fallen at the first hurdle.

Eventually one arrived that *did* fit through the front door. (We struggled down the corridor and into the lounge, but that's another story). There it stood, all magnificent and proud. Like a lion, but with handles, a TV screen and a running board attached. The nice man who delivered it proudly showed me how to fold it up when it wasn't in use (strange that was the first thing he showed me!) and then all he had to do was plug it in and show me what the beast could do.

Problem.

No power cord.

The nice man was embarrassed and promised me that one would be sent to me straight away. So there it stood, my proud fitness lion, minus a tail.

Next Tuesday afternoon, the postman arrived with a special delivery.

IT WAS THE POWER CORD.

Honestly, I hadn't been this excited for ages. I plugged it in and watched its lights light up like a kind of running-machine Christmas tree. Then it was straight into the bedroom to put on my dusty old running clothes.

I stood on my new machine, wearing a tight T-shirt, ill-fitting running shorts and the only trainers I could find that looked like they were for running. I took a deep breath and pressed start, and then:

A BLOODY POWER CUT!

My treadmill had overloaded the circuit and my fuseboard had shut down all the sockets in the room.

After I had fixed that little problem, I was ready to run, and run I did. I ran like the wind blowing through a summer's meadow. Did I balls! Although I did run for quite a decent length of time: 27 minutes and 59 seconds to be precise. I know this because I was keeping notes. (I told you in the first book that I'm quite a sad person.) The next day I ran for 35 minutes. By the end of my first week I had clocked up a very respectable two hours of running.

The following week I did it again. I ran four half-hour sessions and clocked up over ten miles of running nowhere. I lost two and a half pounds and felt very pleased with myself. In fact, pleased isn't the word; SMUG would be a better one. So, as I type this I am now finally back to a decent exercise schedule and looking forward to a brand new me. I just hope ITV doesn't offer me a new TV show filmed in a pub.

GUEST DIARY BITS:
Part 1

24 August
JAMES NESBITT

James Nesbitt was in the studio today. I love him. He's such a great actor and you just know that a night on the beers with him would be a right laugh. What's nice about him is he seems to really like being in the studio with us. Some guests genuinely enjoy listening to the show, so when they come in the studio, they are excited. Jimmy, however, is a great liar! Don't get me wrong, I'm sure he does enjoy it when he's in the studio, but I don't think he listens to the show when he's not on it. But hey, he's a great actor so I can believe that he listens, even though I'd put money on it that he's probably never up before

11am! I also feel that now I am in that exclusive club of people able to call him 'Jimmy' because we are showbiz friends. Remember the definition of showbiz friends is:

"You never call them or see them socially, but if you bump into each other, you can both say hello and hug as if you are proper friends."

RATING: 32.5 OUT OF 40

12 September
WILL FERRELL

I'd seen 'Anchorman' and liked that movie, but it wasn't until he came in today that I 'got' just how funny he is. Although I gotta be honest, both Dave and I were also bloody funny too. He was in to promote his new movie 'Talladega Nights — The Ballad of Ricky Bobby'. Often the movie companies INSIST that we see a film before an actor comes in to promote it. We couldn't all make the screening of this film so I was lucky enough to get sent a video copy instead. Very cool This is quite rare, and I always feel honoured when they actually send you a copy of a film that isn't released yet. It's like having a legal pirate video. Unfortunately, a few friends ended up in my local last night so I had to check to see if they were OK. By the time I was satisfied they were, it was too late to watch the film, so I had a quick watch of it before the show this morning. I often say it's a weird job I have, and I thought this again today at 6.15am as I was trying to watch a 90-minute movie in 45 minutes! Once again I tried to get a part in a big movie by convincing him that we could write a movie about him that also starred me, Dave, Rachel and the rest of the team. He seemed interested, but as yet, hasn't committed.

RATING: 35 OUT OF 40

18 SEPTEMBER
DAVID BECKHAM

I've met David a couple of times before. The first time was back when I was presenting the Saturday morning show. Victoria Beckham was booked as a guest on the show that day and when she turned up, Rachel almost had a heart attack.

'Oh my God, she's here but you'll never guess what. She's here, and so is David and Brooklyn. It's the whole family!' She was very excited.

The second time was when I was in Portugal for the Euro 2004 football tournament. I was lucky enough to go to the England hotel to see my mate Paul Robinson on one of their 'Friends and Family' nights. That was odd, watching all these famous footballers and their families just hanging out, having some food and catching up. We were sitting down to a buffet meal when Victoria sat down at our table with David. 'You know Chris, don't you, David?' said Victoria, although I do think she was telling him rather than asking him.

But today was the first time he'd been on our show, and everybody was buzzing. The first thing I noticed was how nervous he seemed. Not scared, he looked like he wanted to be there, he just seemed a bit nervous. He later told me he had NEVER done a radio show like ours before. He had done interviews with people, but never sat as a guest for an hour just hanging out. He brought me a signed Real Madrid Beckham shirt, which was fucking cool, and a load of other stuff for us to give away. But the best thing was his honesty. I asked him a lot of questions, such as what is a typical day and how does he juggle all his work commitments with his football time. He's a very famous man and seemed a lot more likeable in real life. I told him there would be a place for him at Leeds United if he fancied coming home. I don't think he'll take me up on the offer.

RATING: 35.5 OUT OF 40

26 SEPTEMBER
IAN WRIGHT

Sophie is a massive Arsenal fan and loves Ian Wright. She loves him so much that to her he isn't Ian Wright. He's 'Ian Wright Wright Wright!' Once again the interview got off to a great start. Ian was presenting a new TV show called **'Ian Wright's Unfit Kids'**. In the show he took a load of fat kids and tried to teach them about eating healthily. Ian and I were at it straight away.

'I'm worried about the amount of times you use the word <u>fat</u> though, Chris,' said Ian.

'But these kids are fat!' I replied.

I then explained that even though I was fat, I was also massively good-looking.

'But what about people who aren't as good-looking as you?' asked Ian.

'Get on the radio!' I yelled back. 'All those fat kids on your show.'

'Overweight kids!' Ian yelled back at me.

'Whatever. Look I understand, Ian is trying to re-educate people and I think that it's very commendable,' I said. Then I shoved a huge sausage sandwich into my mouth. Ian started laughing.

'What are you doing?' he screamed.

'Listen, you said on the show, try to stay away from crisps, but you never said anything about a sausage baguette with tommy sauce!'

Before he left he promised that not only would he train me for a week, but also take Sophie to watch the Arsenal one week at the new stadium. Not a bad morning.

RATING: 36 OUT OF 40

27 September
LILY ALLEN

Oh dear. This was a feisty interview. Firstly, I know a lot of guests get nervous before they come on the show. Why not? After all, not only am I a brilliant interviewer, but we've also got a lot of people listening. Secondly, Lily is young and doesn't seem to care about trying to impress people, or so I thought anyway. I don't think she meant to be, but some people found her a bit arrogant. Now I LOVE her album, and I think I like her too, but during the hour-long interview she managed to piss off Comedy Dave — never a good idea — and Producer Rachel. When Rachel introduced herself to Lily before the show, Rachel thought Lily was rude. (I don't know what she was expecting cos I'm never a barrel of laughs when I first wake up!) Anyway, you know when something like this happens, it's going to be a great bit of radio and I couldn't wait.

Within a few minutes of the interview starting, she says: 'Can we get more interesting cos the clock is ticking and I want this to be fun.'

The studio suddenly felt very uncomfortable.

'I'm going,' said Aled as he actually left the room.

Then she says: 'Why does it always have to come back to you, always. Whenever I hear you with a guest it's like, let's talk about Chris.'

This got me going. 'Cos it's the Chris Moyles show and who the hell else am I going to talk about. Pope John Paul II?'

Before I even had a chance to punish her, she turned to Dave. 'Your face really does not suit your voice.'

'Does it not?' asked Dave. 'Is that a compliment or what?' he snarled.

'I feel Lily may be losing the room already,' I said.

Now in her defence, I don't think Lily was trying to be a smart arse, I just think she was nervous. Either way, it was a brilliant bit of radio and if I had been listening to it, I wouldn't have switched off. When we went to 'rate the guest', I tried to explain that she might have come across as a bit cocky, when actually I don't think she was. Besides, I reckon that if we met at a party, she would probably let me tongue kiss her!

RATING: 24 OUT OF 40

3 October
KEITH ALLEN
(Lily Allen's dad!)

Now either this was a pure coincidence, or it was a brilliant piece of guest booking. Just days after Lily had been on the show, her dad came in to talk about the new BBC series,

'Robin Hood', in which he plays the Sheriff of Nottingham. I've always liked Keith Allen. I think he's a great actor and very funny.

Keith was immediately in a naughty mood. The very first thing he said was: 'I've been told not to use the "C" word so you'll be called "Dave" from now on.' He looked straight at Comedy Dave.

Aled dived in and tried to stir things up.

'Why is that, Keith? What's the problem with Dave?'

'With Dave? Apparently he was a bit nasty towards my daughter.'

This was going to be so much fun! Actually Keith was cool with everything and he and I had secretly talked before the show about it and I knew that he was going to give Dave a hard time. We began talking about 'Robin Hood', when Keith changed the subject.

'So Comedy Dave, eh?' And he gave Dave an evil look.

'Oh no,' said Dave. 'You're more scary than the sheriff in real life!'

When it was time to rate the guest, I jokingly gave him 4 out of 10 because I'm tough and not scared of him.

RATING: 25.5 OUT OF 40

Dave rated him 7!

10 October
TAKE THAT

I am amazed at the rejuvenation of Take That. I'm even more amazed that most people seem to like them and seem genuinely pleased about their return. I think they're great. Plus it's always handy being pals with good-looking millionaires. We debuted their first single in ten years, 'Patience', and on shows like this with an exclusive like this, we know EVERYBODY will be listening. Thank God it was good. Gary looks even more out of place than he ever did but he's a nice guy. There were even loads of girls outside waiting for them to arrive. Jesus it was just like being back in 1994. It just makes me laugh to think that girls still scream for them. I heard the only thing Gary screams for these days is his hot chocolate before he goes to bed. God bless Take That. Robbie Who?

RATING: 32.7 OUT OF 40

15 November
JOOLS HOLLAND

Today we had such a laugh. Dominic, our top newsman, is known for doing his awful impressions. We love his Jools Holland impression and he does it a lot on the air. So we decided to stitch him up like a kipper. We managed to get Dominic to do his Jools impression and we told him that Aled would walk in and pretend to be Jools. He fell for it. Dominic launched into his impression:

'Ladies and gentlemen, from over here to over there, it's Jools Holland.'

At that point, the REAL Jools Holland walked in and said good morning. Everybody laughed and Dominic came the closest he's ever come to swearing on the air. I can now reveal that Dom almost screamed 'Fuck me!' when he saw Jools walking in. It was priceless. Jools also said that my first book helped him with his piano technique. He told me that his piano stool was too low, and he uses my book to sit on so he can reach the keys. Cheers.

NO RATING. HE WAS ONLY IN TO MAKE DOMINIC BLUSH!

24 November
RUSSELL BRAND

Like a lot of people, I really wasn't sure about Russell when I first saw him. I thought he looked like a scruffy lanky Goth who needed a bloody good wash. But then I saw him do some stand-up at a charity event one evening and he was hilarious. He was so captivating and extremely funny. I hadn't met him properly before today and he was everything I hoped he would be. When you first see him you notice him straight away. He is instantly striking as he's so tall and with his hair and black drainpipe jeans you can't miss him. He was in to promote his new DVD and he was very funny. The interview got off to a great start when Carrie accused him of not washing his hands after he had visited the boys' toilet. Russell explained they were wet BECAUSE he had washed his hands. I knew it would be fun. We had planned for his interview by preparing the 'Long Word Alarm'. This consisted of a siren blasting out with Rhys's voice saying, 'LONG WORD, LONG WORD. WHAT DOES THAT MEAN, RUSSELL?' every time he said a long word. Which he did several times, including superfluous, which, when asked, Russell explained meant 'excessive and unnecessary, more than is required'. So there!

RATING: 36.5 OUT OF 40

27 November
KATIE PRICE & PETER ANDRE

Jesus H Christ. What the fuck is wrong with these two? I have met them a good few times and actually find them charming and engaging. That isn't to say I wouldn't want to stick a shotgun in my mouth and say goodbye to the world if I had to spend more than a few hours in their company. They are exhausting, to say the least. They were in to promote their album but spent most of the interview bitching at each other, which was very funny. I introduced them as 'the lovely Peter Andre and his beautiful, talented wife and breadwinner, Katie Price.' This girl is a sharp cookie. Believe what you want about Katie, but believe me when I tell you she is a great businesswoman and knows how to milk a product and make a shitload of money out of it. God bless her.

After Katie told us she had a tattoo on her 'ninny', I moved on and did the old trick of trying to get them to mention certain words when they appeared later that morning with Phillip and Fern on TV's 'This Morning'.

'I'll give you for example, cauliflower,' I said.

'Oh wicked,' said Katie. 'Yeah, I see what you mean.'

'What, so if she says "cauliflower" I say "smells like ninny"?' said Pete.

'No, Pete, don't be thick. When we're on the telly today, not now, when we're on the telly, somehow we have to say the word they give us,' Katie explained.

'So if they say "cauliflower" I say "ninny"?'

As I said, they are fascinating to watch together, but after an hour, they leave you exhausted. I imagine it's the same feeling you'd have if you spent the night with her. Good fun, but you'd probably need a good sleep afterwards!

RATING: 27 OUT OF 40

14 December
JIMMY CARR

Here's another guest I instantly liked. I think he's one of the funniest men in Britain. He is so quick and his jokes are excellent. He must be one of the best joke writers in the business. A few days before he came on the show, Jimmy had just won his first British Comedy award. We talked about all matter of things, and like most of our interviews, it started to get very silly.

'Where did you put your award?' I asked.

'Well, about twenty seconds after winning it, they took it out of my hands to be engraved, but my other awards are in my downstairs loo.'

'My awards are in the toilet too,' I bragged.

'Of course. Because you don't want to have them on the mantelpiece but you want everyone else to see them,' said Jimmy.

'Actually mine are on my mantelpiece in there.'

'You've got a mantelpiece in your downstairs loo? That's brilliant.'

'I only have a downstairs loo, I don't have an upstairs,' I explained.

'You don't have an upstairs? You live in a bungalow? You're like an old person. Are you in sheltered accommodation? Is there a warden?'

'No! Anyway, so when you're sitting on the toilet having a poo in my house, which you are more than welcome to do, then you can see my awards.'

'Thanks very much. That's such a kind offer. Often you go on radio shows, they don't even mention whether you could defecate in their house!'

RATING: 31.6 OUT OF 40

19 January
MARY LYNN RAJSKUB

If you watch the TV series '24', then you might recognise this little lady as Chloe. She assists Jack Bauer from her desk at CTU. That's the counter-terrorist unit, of course. We joked about all the stock phrases that get used on the show and about the fact that her character seems to say 'I'm kinda busy right now' in every single episode. During the interview Aled stuck his hand in the air.

'I'd just like to say that I was in 24 once. It was a big scene.'

'What was your job in 24, Aled?' I said, mocking.

'I answered the phone,' he proudly announced.

'Didn't you coordinate a satellite while you were there?' asked Mary Lynn.

I started laughing. 'That's my favourite line of the show so far today. You should get a T-shirt made up. You could use that to get out of boring conversations. "I'm so sorry I've really got to go off and coordinate a satellite. Bye."'

'I'm opening a socket now as we speak!' added Aled.

Now if you don't watch '24' this means nothing to you, so watch it and then read this bit again and I promise you'll laugh.

RATING: 32.7 OUT OF 60

(on our new full team rating system)

7

LIVING ON MY OWN & ORDERING PIZZA

remember one day when I was at school the teacher trying to make a point about how, even though it was nice to spend time with friends and family, it was also nice to spend time on your own. How it was nice to get away from our brothers and sisters sometimes for a bit of peace and quiet. I put my hand up and disagreed. I was never a loner. I loved other people's company. I would rather be with a group of friends then sitting on my own doing nothing. My brother Kieron was the complete opposite. He LOVED spending time on his own. Or maybe he just loved spending time away from his irritating younger brother – who knows? Me, though, I needed people around me, and I was always with other people.

Then, in 1992, at the ripe old age of eighteen, I went to Luxembourg to work for, strangely enough, Radio Luxembourg. I moved into a smart, tiny flat and had to come to terms with spending a lot of time on my own. At first I found it daunting, but as time went on I got used to my own company. Not that I still didn't prefer being with mates, but I suddenly found that being on my own of an evening was a chance for me to do whatever I wanted. I could watch a crap action movie of my choice. I could sit and play on the computer for a few hours. (Note that I said computer. Xbox was a world away in 1992!) As the years passed I pretty much always lived on my own. I was used to it and it really didn't bother me. Occasionally I would be round at a friend's house when their flatmate would come home and I'd wonder if maybe I should get a flatmate for the extra company and a bit of a laugh. But then you go back to your own place and can do whatever you want, because there's nobody there to piss off!

So now I live in London with Sophie, but she still spends time away so there's always a couple of nights a week when it's just me. Now this isn't a problem until it comes to ordering food. A few years ago one of the local pizza places did a two-for-one offer. Now, I'm a working-class Northerner, I couldn't turn a deal like this down.

'Hello, Pizza Pizza, how may I help you?'

This has always struck me as an odd question. You're a pizza delivery company, have a wild stab in the dark as to why I might be calling!

'Yeah, I'd like to order a pizza for delivery please.'

I am always polite when it comes to ordering food. Being sarcastic might slow the food-delivery process down.

'What pizza would you like?'

'I'll have a meat mountain, please.'

'Certainly, and what size would you like, sir?'

Here's the first problem. I'm on my own, but I am very hungry.

However, a large pizza is quite frankly enough for even me. That said, I could eat some of it tonight and then save some for tomorrow for lunch. Genius idea.

'I'll have a large, please.'

There you go, done.

'We have a special offer at the moment, sir, two pizzas for the prize of one. Would you like a second pizza free?'

Oh dear. If I were a normal human being, I would tell him that I didn't need an extra large pizza for free. I would explain that much as this seemed to be excellent value for money, sadly on this occasion, as the food was just for one person, me, it would be wasteful and indeed greedy to order another large meat mountain pizza.

But I don't actually say that.

My hunger for food together with the beer in my belly has turned me into the ultimate greedy bastard. Plus, did I hear the man correctly? Another pizza for free? Granted his English may not be the best, but then why should it, he works for a pizza place, not the bloody United Nations. But yes I was indeed correct, they were practically giving them away. Besides, who am I to turn down their most generous of offers? I wouldn't want to offend the man, let alone the entire marketing and strategy department of the Pizza Pizza Company.

Damn it, I'll take the second free pizza!

But hold on. This does make me seem incredibly greedy. Yes I am a bit drunk and yes I am hungry, but I'm on my own. How can one person justify ordering two large pizzas for himself? That was the point, and I couldn't escape it. The answer was that I couldn't justify it. No matter how greedy I was, I couldn't order another large pizza just for me. I decided to ask for the one pizza, but as I opened my mouth to answer his question, the demon inside me awoke and began talking for me.

'Two for one, you say. Hold on a second, please, mate.'

I pull the phone away from my mouth and shout to the other room.

'Hey, lads, it's two for one. Shall we get another pizza for free?'

Oh My God! What am I doing? Am I really pretending there are other people here, just so the guy at the pizza place doesn't think I'm a greedy bastard? I can't believe I'm doing this.

'Yeah, go on then, mate, why not, it will get eaten.'

What is wrong with me? I am pretending to talk to flatmates I don't have in order to fool a man whose job it is to answer the phones at Pizza Pizza into thinking that I don't live on my own and therefore I am not greedy.

Then, it actually gets worse.

Half an hour later the doorbell rings. I have gone to all this trouble to convince the person on the phone at the pizza place, but now we have another problem. The person on the other side of the door is the delivery guy. I can't have *him* thinking I am a greedy loner who sits in at night and eats two large pizzas back to back. So the demon is released again, and I can't believe that I'm doing this. As I walk to the door and begin to open it, I launch into conversation with my imaginary flatmates.

'No, it's fine, I'll be back in a minute, hang on.'

I open the door as I'm saying this and pay the delivery guy. Then as I am closing the door, I start again.

'Hey, lads, the pizzas are here!'

Just loud enough for the delivery guy, who couldn't care less, to hear me and therefore know that I am not alone and not a greedy bastard.

It's pathetic, I know, and I'm embarrassed.

Could I possibly sink lower than that?

Well yes, actually.

Occasionally the man on the phone will ask:

'Would you like any desserts, sir?'

Aaaaaarrrrgggggh!

8

AN EXPLANATION

I'd like to take a few paragraphs now away from the book to clear something up.

As you read through what I have written, you may have noticed that the word 'beer' appears a few times. As does the word 'pub'.

Please now allow me to explain the frequent usage of these words.

I LOVE BEER AND I LOVE THE BLOODY PUB!

That's it.

I don't have a drink problem, although I will admit to having a beer-retention problem. I just love the crack of being in the pub with my mates. I know a lot of people think I'm hanging out with the rich and famous, but I'm not. Normally I sit in my local with a few pals and we either catch up on what we're all up to, or we just talk shite like everybody else. Sometimes I like to hold court, like those annoying fat people who won't shut up with their bloody stories, but other times I just sit there and listen to somebody else spouting their stories. Either way, it's great and I love it.

My local pub is typical. The people are friendly and the toilets are disgusting. I always feel that is the key to a good pub. If I ever go somewhere else and find that the toilets are friendly, I leave straight away. You just know that the people in there will be trouble.

When it comes to lavatory visits, by the way, I can last a few drinks before going, but when you do decide to visit the boys' room, that's it. It's all over. As Comedy Dave says:

'Once you pop, you just can't stop.'

Anyway, it's a pub and I don't want the toilets looking better than the toilet in my own home, and trust me, in my local, they don't. They're on a par with the public toilets in the park that you only ever use in an emergency. Actually there was a time when we used to use the toilet as part of our amusement. For no reason that I recall, it became a regular thing for people to throw coins into the urinal. It was like some kind of dirty wishing well. Or 'Pissing Well' as I called it. It was the normal pennies and five- or ten-pence pieces. One night, just for a laugh, we decided to throw a few two-pound coins in there, give them a good soaking, and then sit and watch as people went in and out for a piss. After each person left, one of us would run in and check to see if the two-pound coins were still in there. Unbelievably, it took less than five minutes for the coins to disappear. And just on the off-chance that the person who took them is reading this: we saw you leave and we know who you are. Pissy fingers!

The decor in the pub is unique also. There's of course the usual 'memorabilia' on the wall. None of which has anything to do with the name of the pub, its location or customers. My favourite is a glass box of tennis memorabilia from about fifty years ago. Why? I have no idea.

The walls were once green in colour. Now they are a kind of dark green with an added smoky effect. Or at least they were until the smoking ban came in, when they decided to have a 'refit'. You and I would call it 'a lick of paint', but who am I to argue? I love the place all the same.

The only problem is – well, in fact, there are a few problems with my love of the pub.

First, if I have nothing better to do with my time, or if I have no plans or commitments for the day, I can sit in there for hours. I mean it, hours. Get in at four o'clock and sit there till ten o'clock at night. It's not a problem for me, as I am a social drinking machine. Sophie finds this amazing.

'What the hell do you talk about in a pub for that long?' she will ask.

'Nothing' is normally my reply.

And it's true. My pals and me sit there and talk nonsense to each other for hours. Now, of course, the drink helps. I mean, I'm sure some of my mates are a lot more boring in real life than what they seem like after six pints of weak lager, but they are, on the whole, a funny bunch of people.

There's my mate Kevin who pops into the pub on his way home from work. He does this virtually every night of the week. His wife must think he works in Glasgow as it takes him two hours from leaving the office to walking through the front door. Kevin is a man who knows everything. Apart from the fact that drinking pints of strong lager makes you slur your words and talk rubbish!

There's a Greek bloke called Harry, or 'Arry, as we all seem to call him. He's a very likeable, jolly character who has a big beard and drives a nice car. I've never been sure exactly what he does but he often buys me a drink so I don't think that I should ask! Normally when I see him he will utter his catchphrase. He's not famous, but he does have a catchphrase.

'Hello, Chris. Let's get drunk.'

He says this in his London Greek accent. The only thing wrong with this is that he never does get drunk. He is a drinking machine. He'll stand at the bar talking to you and enjoying his drinks and you can never tell if he's had one or fifteen, so as catchphrases go, it's not that accurate for him.

In fact, a few people in the pub have their own catchphrase. Andy is another very jolly character. He always seems to be laughing. I mean constantly. And he looks like Errol Brown, lead singer with the band Hot Chocolate. There have been many nights when I have convinced a drunk friend that he was indeed the man himself, as Andy will break into 'You Sexy Thing' right on cue.

Then there is our beloved landlord, Andrew. He's an Irish man who has run the pub for years. He is very lovely and has a strong accent. However, sometimes he can be a tad moody, which is why his catchphrase is:

'You're barred!'

Screamed in his thick gravelly Irish accent. He has other catch-phrases too, including:

'Fuck off!'

'No!'

and the hilarious:

'Just to let you know that the bar is still open!'

This is usually when he thinks you're not spending enough money in there. God forbid you ever pop in just to use the toilets. On those occasions you will get to hear variations of 'Fuck off!' and all manner of others I couldn't possibly put in this book.

Then there's Tim, who I used to work with. I see him quite a bit and he's a good lad. He does seem to have quite an unhealthy name-dropping habit. He also seems to think that I know every famous person in the world, and has an obsession with shortening their names.

'I saw Sadie earlier,' he'll say.

'Sadie who?' I'll ask.

'Sadie. Sadie Frost.'

'Tim, you do know I've never met Sadie Frost, don't you?'

One day we were all sitting chatting and having a drink, just catching up, when Tim suddenly said:

'I was out with Rupes earlier.'

Sophie and I looked at each other.

'Rupes? Who the hell is Rupes?' I asked.

'Rupert,' replied Tim, as if he was referring to a guy sitting next to us.

'Rupert?' I started to rack my brains. 'I don't think I know a Rupert,' I said.

'Yeah you do. Rupert. Will Young's brother.'

'Will Young's brother? What the hell are you talking about? How the hell are we supposed to know Will Young's brother, let alone know him well enough to call him Rupes?'

'Well you know Will, don't you?' said Tim.

'Well yeah, I do, but I don't know his brother. Just because you meet somebody doesn't mean you know the whole family. I've met Gareth Gates as well but I don't know his bloody mother, do I?'

'I've never met Gareth Gates,' said Tim, looking confused.

'Never mind, Tim. Rupes my arse!'

Another time I was meeting up with my old friend Richard Bacon. We had become pals after he got sacked from *Blue Peter* after newspaper allegations that he'd been a naughty boy. We spent a lot of time together but hadn't seen each other for a while, so we were meeting for a good old-fashioned catch-up. When I got to the pub, Tim was in there with more of my mates. I explained that I was meeting Richard, as a few of the guys hadn't seen him for ages either.

'Who's that? Richard Bacon?' asked Tim.

'Yeah, he's on his way for a pint.'

'Where does he work now? I haven't heard him for ages.'

'He's still at Capital Radio, doing the afternoon shift,' I explained.

'I wouldn't know,' said Tim. 'I never listen to him.'

'You should, he's very good.'

I went to the bar to get a round in and Richard turned up. He put his order in and sat down next to Tim. As I was walking back to the group with the beers I heard Tim chatting to Richard.

'You still at Capital, Rich?' Once again, shortening his name.

'Yeah yeah. Just finished at seven tonight.'

Tim leaned in to him. 'Love the show by the way. It's really great.'

The two-faced cheeky bastard. I kept quiet until later when Richard went to the toilet. For a piss, I must add, he wasn't being naughty again. I looked at Tim.

'You're a little piss-taker, you are. You told me you didn't listen to him.'

Tim took a sip of his pint and looked at me with a big smile. 'I don't. But I'm hardly going to tell him that he's shit, am I?' And he started laughing.

I love Tim. He's a funny bloke.

So, yes, I love hanging out in my local pub. Plus it's not like I do this every single day of the week. It might not even be once a week if

I'm busy. However, if Sophie is away for the night then I might meet up with a pal for a couple of pints in the late afternoon. Then another mate might turn up so we have a few more. Then some more friends might pop in later, by which time we may as well stay for another!

Another problem with the pub is what I drink. Lager, and lots of it. After years and years of drinking the stuff, it has finally occurred to me that this may be the cause of my beer belly. Really? Yes. I now believe that all that lager going into my tummy has helped me to become fat. And then when I get home after drinking lots of beer, I might as well have a Chinese delivered and start my fitness campaign tomorrow!

I do, however, get a hell of a lot of material from the pub. And it's just a normal pub. It's not anything special at all. Remember what I said about the toilets, for God's sake. There's hardly any plaster left on the ceiling and I'm sure there's an animal of some sorts rotting behind the cistern.

At the moment I have no kids and I'm not married. Should this change then I am sure I will spend less time drinking with my mates down the local. It will, however, also mean that my next book will be about changing nappies and how I don't ever leave the house any more. That'll be one hell of a read!

JAMIE REDKNAPP ON MOYLES

Chris Moyles, when you listen to him on the radio and meet him, you think he has cracked it! But my wife Louise told me when he used to work on local radio and their group Eternal turned up to meet him, he used to wear shocking silk shirts and sweat profusely!

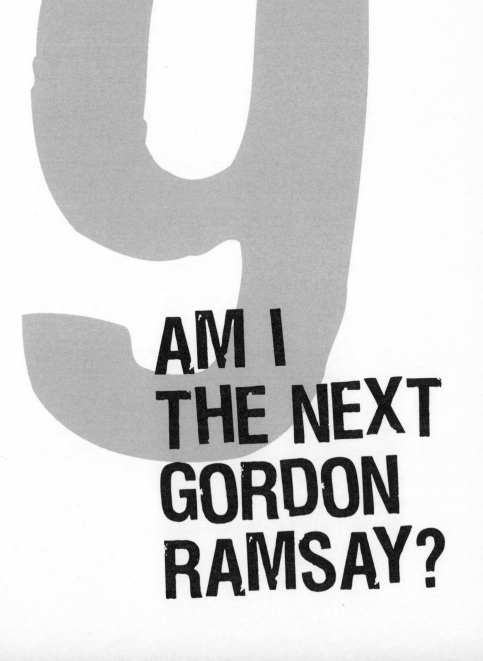

9

AM I THE NEXT GORDON RAMSAY?

Now I know that I should try and tease you into thinking there is more to me than just a bloody great radio broadcaster. Let you into my world a little bit more and share with you my innermost secrets and skills I have never spoken about on the radio. Maybe I am the next Gordon Ramsay, you never know. Perhaps I am secretly a brilliant chef, but I'm too shy to cook for other people for fear of their overwhelming response to my creative and exciting dishes. Well, to answer the question:

AM I BALLS!

I hate cooking. It's boring. Not that I have done enough cooking to actually know that it's boring, but from the little that I have done, it is, pretty much, a boring process. I hate virtually every aspect of it, with the exception of the 'eating' part. I even hate being asked if I cook. The real answer is no, I don't cook. I can't cook. I really am the 'can't cook, won't cook' typical man. Of course, I can do some 'things' in the kitchen, such as 'heating up' or 'sticking in the oven'. Matt Lucas and I were discussing this subject one day and he summed it up perfectly:

'If I take something and pop it into the microwave, I am preparing food. If I take it out of the freezer and stick it in the oven for half an hour, then that to me is cooking!'

I have argued this point with my friends for years. If I am hungry, I can cook, or prepare, many different dishes. You want some pasta? I can do that for you. Fancy a garlic bread starter? No problem, give me twenty minutes. My main dish is chicken pie and chips. This is my specialty. If you want a detailed recipe, then knock yourself out with this.

PÂTÉ EN CROUTE ET POMMES CHIPS DE POULET

(I stuck 'chicken pie and chips' into a translator website. God knows what it says!)

Take a Bird's Eye chicken pie and place in a preheated
oven at 200°C.
Cook for 10 minutes.
Add some frozen oven chips.
Cook for 10 minutes.
Turn the chips over.
Cook for a further 10 minutes, or until golden brown.
Remove from the oven, serve and eat.

Now if that isn't cooking, then I don't know what is!

I also do various dishes that include bread or toast, but after several arguments with friends I have sadly come to the conclusion that this is called 'making a sandwich' and consequently doesn't count for shit.

So I suppose the bottom line of it is that I do not cook.

Mind you, I don't often have to. I go out to eat a lot and have even been to a couple of posh fancy restaurants that are owned by famous people. When I got the breakfast show on Radio 1, Sophie wanted to take me out somewhere special. She knew it was my dream job so she wanted to go somewhere cool. It's weird how when Sophie wants to take me somewhere as a treat, it's almost always somewhere that SHE'S wanted to go to for ages. So she decided that Jamie Oliver's Fifteen restaurant was the place to go. Complete coincidence that she's been banging on about going for dinner there for months. So she called them up and tried to book a table.

'I'm afraid we're booked up for the next six months,' said the lady on the phone.

'Six months?' yelled Sophie.

'Yes, madam. We are taking dates from March next year.'

'I was kind of hoping for tomorrow night.'

'Sorry, madam,' came the reply.

Sophie put the phone down feeling very disappointed. Suddenly, she picked the phone back up and pressed redial. The same woman answered.

'Hello, may I help you?'

'Oh hello. My name is Sophie and I'm calling from the Radio 1 press office. I'd like to book a table for one of our DJs, Chris Moyles, and his girlfriend, please.'

At this point Sophie realised what she was saying. Not only did she not work for the press office at Radio 1, she didn't even work for Radio 1! Yet here she was on the telephone lying about who she was to a woman she's just spoken to, in order to book a table at a restaurant she knew was booked up for the next six months. She's never done anything like this before. Ever. The woman on the end of the phone is only going to tell her that they're booked up.

'Certainly, madam, what night would you like to come?'

RESULT!

Sophie booked the table and immediately called Julian in the Radio 1 press office.

'Julian, it's Sophie. I've just done something really embarrassing,' she said.

Julian is a good friend of ours so luckily he found it funny and Sophie promised never to do it again.

Now if you think you've just found a way of getting a table in a booked-up restaurant of your choice, don't bother. Let me tell you that it's not worth trying as this NEVER usually works. One day I called a restaurant and tried to book a table. I was told they had nothing for three weeks. Remembering Sophie I called back and tried again, but this time I said I was Chris Moyles calling from BBC Radio 1.

'Sir, as I told you when you called the first time, we don't have anything for the next three weeks.'

I never did it again.

Anyway, back to food.

One of the reasons I don't cook is I am too lazy. Laziness is a huge factor in my life. I don't cook because I am too lazy to try, too lazy to wait for it to cook, and too lazy to wash up afterwards. (I am also too lazy to learn an instrument, too lazy to get myself back in shape – although this I am working on, kind of – and too lazy to discover a cure for the common cold.) Another reason for my lack of culinary skills is that I have funny eating habits. Or so people tell me. When they tell me I'm a fussy eater, I tell them they are talking bollocks. But I will admit that, yes, **there are a few things I don't eat, such as onions, mushrooms, tomatoes and cheese**, but that's not a massive problem.

OK, so **these ingredients are used in almost every single bloody dish on the planet,** making me a nightmare to go for dinner with.

Anyway, if I want a Chinese dish, then it is just one phone call and twenty minutes away from sitting on a plate in front of me, so my not cooking is not a problem for me. It is, however, a problem for EVERYBODY else. Sophie says I should learn to cook. My mum says I should learn to cook. And now, Gordon Ramsay has said I should learn to cook.

I met Gordon when he came on the radio show to promote his book, but I was more interested in asking him about his menus. I had wanted to go for dinner at one of his restaurants for a while. Sophie had been bugging me for ages to take her, but the truth was I was scared I wouldn't even understand the menu. So now that I had Gordon in front of me, live on the radio, I decided I would ask him to take me through one of his typical menus. I chose his restaurant Gordon Ramsay at Claridge's, asking him, 'Is that a good one?' The man has been awarded about ten Michelin stars and I'm asking him if this is a good one! He called me a pleb.

I then went through the set lunch menu and ripped apart the dishes.

'Right, Gordon, desserts. Fig and almond tart with a fragola grape sorbet. Waste of time. Nobody's gonna have that. Granny Smith apple parfait and donuts, bingo. That's all you need.'

He laughed a lot but I could tell he thought I was a nightmare.

'I'll come to your place one day, but I'd love to take you out for lunch,' I told him.

'OK. Where are we going to go?' I had him hooked.

'I will take you to a place called the Marathon Kebab Shop in Camden, North London.' I was trying to sell him the idea of proper food.

'Is it a takeaway?' asked Gordon.

'Yeah, or you can eat in.' I thought he might be coming round to my way of thinking. I was wrong.

'You're such a pleb,' was his response.

I always thought this place was like Kebab Heaven. Gordon didn't seem interested!

As well as being a food genius, he also has his own TV show called *The F Word*, the F standing for 'food' and also for the fact that he says the word 'FUCK' a hell of a lot. Now I can swear, let me tell you, but this guy is something else. My radio team and I visited the F Word restaurant for dinner one night. As I have said before, we get some great perks working on the radio, and this was no exception. Turn up at the restaurant and sit down for dinner. Eat the free food that has been prepared for us and drink the free drinks. At some point Gordon will come over to the table and have a 'little chat' with me and ask me if I liked the food. Repeat this for the main course and dessert, then go home. What a deal. What I didn't know was that I had been set up. Gordon had found out that I liked my Indian food so much that I had my local curry house phone number in my mobile. (He told me he was appalled that I had it on speed dial. This was a downright lie. It was not on speed dial. But I did have AAA before the name so it came up on my address list first!)

He called them and asked if Chris Moyles was one of their customers.

'Yes, Mr Moyles is one of our regular customers. He uses us a few times a week.'

'A few times a week?' screamed Gordon. This was embarrassing.

Gordon then asked the guy what I normally ordered.

'I think he likes chicken curry with no onions.'

Jesus Christ, he remembers I don't like onions.

'He has pilau rice and some poppadoms to start.'

Shit, this guy's like a memory machine.

'And he also orders a kema naan.'

Oh please shut the fuck up.

Everybody round the table was laughing and Gordon's face looked disgusted. He then ordered all the food and told the guy to deliver it to the restaurant we were all sat in. Then Gordon dragged ME into his kitchen and told me that together we were going to COOK my very own curry in the time it would take my local place to deliver theirs. Now I love curry, but I can't cook one. And I certainly can't cook stood next to Gordon Fucking Ramsay. That said, he told me what to do and I did it. Twenty minutes later and I had made my first-ever curry. With a little help from an award-winning world-renowned chef, of course. Gordon made me promise never to order a curry from my local place ever again, and in future to make the curry myself.

I went home that night delighted with myself. Even Sophie was proud of me. So we celebrated by ordering a Chinese takeaway.

WELL, AT LEAST IT WASN'T A CURRY.

10
WRITING A BOOK

would like now to take you through the process of putting this book together. I'm aware there will be a few people reading this who have aspirations to write their own book – to one day sit down and pen their very own bestseller. Good luck to you, I say, but please don't use me as an example. The thought of me, Chris Moyles, actually being an inspiration to these people is as ridiculous as Dale Winton being a pin-up poster for a teenage girl, though stranger things have happened. Most of you reading this book, however, will be merely interested in what I have to say. Or you will have been given this book as a gift. Or you will be currently sitting on your friend's toilet and have picked up the copy they probably got as a gift themselves. Either way I would like to give you an insight into the amazing world of book publishers.

When I started out on this 'author' journey (or 'awful' journey, depending on what your take is) I never imagined how ridiculous my life would at times become. One afternoon I'd be sitting at home playing Call of Duty 2 on Xbox live, being shot at by a German controlled by a 15-year-old spotty boy in Texas; the next afternoon I'd be in a meeting discussing the title of the book and indeed having a row over what it should be called.

The reason I'm having these arguments is simple.

You see, I could have chosen an easy way to write this book. A simple and effective formula that has been used hundreds of times before in what is known, and what I have grown to hate, as the Celebrity Book World. For Chris Moyles, however, nothing is easy. My life is constantly filled with complications. Everyday simple tasks are turned into American-TV-style dramas. Washing up for you may take a quick few minutes, but not for me. Every individual knife has to be washed, stroked and rubbed with a cloth, rinsed of its suds and then carefully wiped and dried to ensure it is absolutely 100 per cent clean. I can't just wash it and leave it to dry – are you mad? That would create 'sud stains' on the knife, making it look like it hasn't been washed at all. (Now you understand why I have a cleaner!)

Perhaps you're going on a long journey in the car and fancy listening to some music while you drive. Putting the radio on would be an option, or even sticking a CD in the CD player. Not for me. I have to sit down at my laptop, buy some music from iTunes and create a compilation CD that contains appropriate music for my destination or reason for travelling. I also have to give the CD a fucking name:

Going to the Leeds festival

Ipswich versus Leeds – the journey home

Sad? Yes, I admit it, but as I always say when I embarrass myself by admitting something like this, I know I'm not the only one!

So when it came to writing this book I chose yet another awkward path. Not only was this route difficult, but it is also fairly rare, and in some circles almost unheard of.

I AM WRITING THE BOOK MYSELF.

To me there was no discussion about getting in a ghostwriter. I am the only one who knows what is going on in my head and even I have trouble with that most of the time. Most books written by so-called celebrities are not written by the so-called celebrity themselves, but by a ghostwriter. Often the ghostwriter gets a credit, like 'Written by Celebrity Name and Mike Johnson'. Mike Johnson may have sat down with the celeb and chatted with them about their lives, but then he would have gone away and written every word of the book. (I met a celeb one day who told me not only had they not written their autobiography, but they had not even read it!)

No, that way round wasn't for me. I had to write it myself, and because I am also an egotistical control freak, I also have to be involved in EVERY other aspect of the book too, from writing it to what bloody shelf it sits on in the bookshop. But then again, how could I not be involved? It's a book, about me, with my face on the front cover. I genuinely can't understand somebody who will let a book appear about them, and not be involved in the process of it. Actually, I take that back. There are SOME stupid, self-obsessed, untalented, fame-craving idiots who think this is EXACTLY the way it should work, but I'm not one of them.

So, with all this in mind, I find myself sitting at home with Miranda, my editor, as we discuss what this book is going to be about. I throw a few ideas at her and she tells me which ones she likes. It's all going well until she shows me some 'rough' ideas for the front cover.

Earlier we had had a discussion about the title of the book. Now I wanted to call it 'The Difficult Second Book'. This made Miranda chuckle so I thought we had agreed. However, as I say, nothing is ever simple in my life.

'What about the subtitle?' she asks.

Cue problem number 1.

My publishers have way more experience than I have in the book world, so of course I'm going to trust them. However, I have some ideas and I think they are good ideas. And yes, Miranda likes my title, but it's not enough. My publishers are OBSESSED with subtitles. To them a book can't be called *Something*. It has to be *Something – A story of some thing*.

Go to any bookshop and you can spot the books published by my publishers. They all have a title AND a bloody subtitle.

LOSE WEIGHT – A book about how to lose weight.

Or:

MY LIFE STORY – The story of my life.

Or:

THE BIBLE – A story of one man and many fish.

They are obsessed with subtitles and I knew that I had to give them one (ooh er!).

'Ok, how about: *The Difficult Second Book, cashing in on the success of the first*,' I said.

'You can't do that!' said Miranda.

'Why not?' I asked.

'Well, because that implies you are only doing it for the money.'

(And people say I'm stupid!)

'It's not that, I just think it's a funny title,' I explained.

'No, that's not good enough,' she told me.

So I went away and tried to think of another title to go with the title that we both liked.

'How about: *The Secret Diary of Chris Moyles*. That's a good one,' she said.

I looked at her in amazement. 'Are you serious?'

'Yeah, why, what's wrong with that? I like it,' she proclaimed.

'Well, in case it has slipped your mind, I'm sure that particular title has been used quite successfully before.'

'*The Secret Diary of Chris Moyles*?'

'No, smart arse. *The Secret Diary of Adrian Mole*. That was kind of a big-selling brand a few years ago.'

'Yeah I know it was, but that's the joke.'

I wasn't getting it.

'It's a joke that's about twenty years old, for God's sake. I may as well call the book *The Bible Part 3*!'

'Oh, that's just silly.'

Silly maybe, but at least we would've had some sales from religious nutters, and who knows, maybe they'd've thought I was the second coming. Imagine that. You'd probably eat for free and get off loads of parking tickets.

So the row went on until Miranda came round to mine one day to show me the new 'rough' covers for the book.

'Why does it say *The Secret Diary of Chris Moyles* on the cover?' I could feel myself getting mad.

'Well, I know you're not keen on that title, but—'

'NOT KEEN!' I shouted. 'It's not that I'm *not keen*. I'm *not keen* on carrots. I'm *not keen* on cruise holidays. This isn't *not keen*, this is me saying I think that title is rubbish!'

'Well, we need a subtitle for the book and so far we don't have one,' she screamed.

'I don't give a shit, but I don't want to call it that. How about: *The Difficult Second Book*, subtitle: *Buy it!* How about that?'

'You can't call it that.'

'I can't believe we're having a row about this!' I yelled.

'We're not having a row about it, we just need to agree the title elements,' said Miranda.

It was at this point that I had one of those out-of-body experiences. You know when you seem to be able to leave your own body, float up into the air and look down on yourself below. Well, I had one of those, and all I could see was me having an 'agreeing the title elements' conversation!

I had a similar conversation about the photo for the cover of my first book, *The Gospel According to...* I thought it would be funny to have a photo of me on the cross like Christ. In one hand I'd have a microphone and in the other a pint of beer. This went down like Michael Barrymore at a swimming-pool convention.

'Look, all I'm saying is that people need to know what the book is about before they buy it,' explained Miranda, who amazingly hadn't lost the will to live by this point.

'But I don't think they do. I think people will either buy it or they won't. It's simple. People who like me might buy it, and people who hate me won't buy it,' said me, an expert already!

'Yes, but even with people who don't like you, we'd like them to buy the book.'

'In that case take my picture off the front cover then,' said me being a smart arse.

'Stop being a smart arse,' she said.

This is another thing. Bosses always want me to appeal to every-body, and that's impossible. If somebody doesn't like me, chances are that I cannot change their mind. Now there *is* a good chance that eventually they will come round and start to like the show. This often happens when friends keep telling them how funny the show is, or they know somebody who has met me and was intrigued to find out that I'm actually a nice guy in real life. Word of mouth is the one thing that both puts people off the show AND turns people on to it.

So here we were at a crossroads. Miranda wants the cover to appeal to people who might not like me, that they may be intrigued enough to pick it up. I, on the other hand, want the cover to be as creative and as 'me' as the rest of the book. It was at this point that I had a wicked idea.

'OK, so you want the word "diary" in the title, so how about this.'

CHRIS MOYLES – THE DIFFICULT SECOND BOOK

My publishers wanted me to include the word 'diary' in the title but sadly there wasn't enough room on the front cov.

BRILLIANT!

This was met with a smile for a few seconds, before the smile turned to a look that Mum used to give me when I hid cabbage under my meat and told her I had eaten it.

'Can I at least have another subtitle so we can choose?' Miranda was now looking as bored with the conversation as I was.

'OK, how about: "*Part diary, part rant, from a part-time famous person.*" How does that grab you?'

Miranda's look now turned into the look of a woman who has just been told that George Clooney was about to walk out of my bathroom naked.

'I actually like that title. I like that a lot.' She was even smiling.

'Thank God. There you go then. Result.'

Together, we had come up with a title for the book, AND a bloody subtitle, which gave an indication of what the book was about, and was still in keeping with my style. We had argued and shouted at each other, but we got there in the end. We were satisfied and relieved, and also we knew that we would probably never have to go through this ordeal ever again. It had taken us three hours to do this and I had gone pale in the face.

Then Miranda looked at me. 'Now, any thoughts for the back cover?'

Jesus, does this shit never end!

Note: As I write, my exasperated publishers are now toying with: *There Is No Subtitle To This Book*.

ANDI PETERS ON MOYLES

I've known Chris for around ten years now (since he worked at Capital). When I say I've known Chris, I mean, since he first slagged me off on Capital!! Me being me, I challenged him, and that's when and how we became friends. Because we both worked at Radio Top Shop, there's a certain respect for each other (I worked in the flagship London branch, he worked in a region). It's funny knowing someone with such a big mouth as you never know what he's going to say, but what I do know is that he is someone I can trust; he'll scare the heck out of you but never betray you and that's what makes him a GOOD FRIEND!!! (He does swear a lot and drink a lot but hey, he's from Leeds.)

11
MY LIFE THROUGH THE BRIT AWARDS

At risk of explaining the glaringly obvious, the Brit Awards is the biggest event in the British music industry's calendar. Each year the finest and often not so finest artists from the past twelve months congregate at one special place in London for an evening of performances, speeches and, most importantly, so it seems to me, drinking. There are of course other things going on that I am blissfully unaware of. A friend of mine recently came back from a skiing holiday. When I quizzed him about the weather he told me he hadn't seen that much white stuff in one place since last year's Brit Awards.

All very rock and roll to the Brit Awards virgin. I was lucky enough to be invited to my first Brits in 1998. I had just turned twenty-four and had been working at Radio 1 for only a few months, so I was as excitable as David Dickinson in a 50%-off tanning salon. My producer at the time, Ben Cooper, and I decided to go out and buy ourselves a new suit and pair of shoes each. After all, this was the coolest awards ceremony we had ever been to. So we trotted off into London town to seek out cool clothes to wear to make us look hip and trendy. Sadly, when you're overweight with shoulder-length hair, as I had in those days, you have to settle for what you can fit into rather than what looks cool.

The awards in 1998 were held at the London Arena, not the easiest of places to get to by car, especially when 5,000 other cars are also heading the same way. I remember sitting in traffic for about two hours, creasing my High and Mighty suit in the process. When we got into the arena, Ben and I were SO excited. We sat down at the special Radio 1 table and tucked into the free food and drink. (I imagine somebody paid for it. I don't know who, but it wasn't us!) Then the lights go down and the show begins.

For those of you who have never been, which I imagine is most of you (I assume you haven't, as most of my mates haven't been either), let me guide you through what it REALLY is like sitting on a table at the Brit Awards.

The first twenty minutes is BRILLIANT. It is so exciting to be there and the atmosphere is electric. The electricity starts to disappear as more and more drunken record-company executives begin to fidget and move round the room, talking loudly to whoever will listen and blowing cigar smoke all over the place. Half an hour in and you wish they would all shut the fuck up and go home. What is the point of going to such a cool night and then getting drunk and talking all the way through it? Get drunk YES but at least watch the fucking show!

It was a good one as well, despite being hosted by Ben Elton, not the coolest man you could've chosen. Mind you, it was before *We Will Rock You*, the so-called Queen musical, so at least that was something. Robbie Williams and Tom Jones performed together, and Chumbawamba famously soaked John Prescott. Rock and indeed Roll.

After the awards are the famous 'after-show parties'. There is always an official party at the venue, but most of the bands head off to their own record company parties in some swish venue somewhere. However, in 1998, when you're on the radio at four o'clock the next morning, it's a search for a cab home and then a short sleep and being back on the air before most of the winners have even gone to bed.

I managed to wangle another invite twelve months later, and realised the night is pretty much exactly the same except with different winners. This was the year that Fatboy Slim won best dance act and accepted his award by holding up a piece of paper that read 'SPEECHLESS'. Robbie Williams won three awards and collected one of his by holding up a piece of paper that read 'LEGLESS'. That was funny. What wasn't so funny that year was my table. I was very excited to have tickets for the event, and when they turned up I was giddy like a child after too much fizzy pop. I opened the envelope to find my Gold tickets sitting inside.

'I've got Gold tickets for the Brits this year,' I told my mate, showing off because obviously I was a big star at Radio 1 now and of course I should have the best tickets available.

'Are they good seats?' he asked.

'Good? What are you talking about? Did you not hear me? I have GOLD tickets. Not bronze, not silver, but GOLD. It's got to be one of the best tables in the room, mate,' I bragged. 'Good isn't the word. The word is GOLD, and what's better than gold?'

I arrived at the venue and located the floorplan to work out just how near the stage our table was. It wasn't next to the stage. It wasn't even near the stage. It was, however, virtually the last table on the floorplan. In fact, the table was so far back in the room, it was like sitting in the bastard car park. I would have had a better view if I'd stood outside Dixon's and watched it on the bloody telly.

What is better than Gold? Platinum, as it turned out!

In 2000 I was there to witness the pop band Five open the show performing their cover of Queen's 'We Will Rock You'. Halfway through, the stage changed to reveal Roger Taylor on the drums and Brian May playing the guitar solo. Ben Elton must have been sitting at home watching the TV and thinking, 'Now that gives me an idea.' So the way I see it, Five are to blame for the sacrilegious Queen musical.

I'd had a lot of fun taking the mickey out of Five at this point. I had been goofing on them on the radio for a while and enjoyed every second of it. J, the 'tough'-looking one, was my favourite to take the piss out of. Here was a guy with a ring through his pierced eyebrow who seemed to think he was a hard-core rapper. He wasn't. He was in the band '5ive'. They actually won an award for Best Pop Act that year. I was sitting at my table chatting to somebody, no doubt some record company executive smoking a cigar, when my friend and colleague Emma B got all excited and screamed at me.

'You just had a mention!'

'I did? From who?' I asked.

'J from Five just said he was going to find you and stick the award where the sun don't shine!'

'Where's that? Cleethorpes?'

'You what?' asked Emma, who actually seemed excited that I had been mentioned on stage at the Brits by J from the boy band Five. Bless her.

This was also the year that Ronnie Wood from the Rolling Stones had an altercation with the DJ Brandon Block. There have been many versions of this story over the years. And this is mine ...

I was chatting with Emma just as the awards had started. (This record-company-chatting thing is contagious, it seems.) I noticed that Brandon, whom I'd never met before, kept looking over to us and giving us a thumbs-up.

'Who the hell is that?' I asked Emma.

'It's Brandon.'

'Brandon who?' I was so down with my dance DJs.

'Brandon Block!' replied Emma.

I'd heard of the guy but didn't know much about him. Moments later he came over and introduced himself. It turned out he really liked the show and so we ended up chatting. (With so many people who don't like the show I have to take what I can get!) He sat on the floor, I remember, drinking out of a bottle of champagne, telling me he'd brought his dad to the awards because he was proud to be nominated for best dance single. Now, Brandon seemed to be getting a little tipsy, so I wrapped up the conversation and headed back to Emma B's side. Not so long after, a guy randomly walked on to the stage in front of a bemused Ronnie Wood.

'Oh my God it's Brandon!' shrieked Emma.

And it was.

Now the story I heard was that Brandon had been sitting on a table chatting to somebody as the winner of another award was read out on the stage. Some joker told Brandon that HE had WON his award and that Ronnie Wood had just read Brandon's name out. The table then urged Brandon to get to the stage to pick it up before it was too late. So what we saw was Ronnie Wood giving out the award for Best Soundtrack to the movie *Notting Hill*, and a drunk DJ wandering on to the stage to collect what he thought was his award.

'Who are you, mate?' asked a confused Ronnie Wood.

'Brandon Block, mate. Oi oi!' came the drunk and loud reply.

Ronnie didn't know what was going on.

Brandon didn't know what was going on.

The show producers didn't even know what was going on.

Eventually Ronnie told Brandon to 'Piss off' and threw a drink over him. It all kicked off. How would Ben Elton have coped with that?

2003 saw a major change for the producers of the Brits TV show. The idea was to broadcast the show 'as live'. Normally the Brits take place the evening before the broadcast, giving the programme makers just enough time to edit out any foul language these naughty drunk musicians have used. I think they also wanted to make the ceremony a little classier. Make the record company people shut up and actually pay attention to what was going on onstage. But the question was: how? How do you make a room full of record company bigwigs, celebrities and rock and pop stars stay quiet and behave themselves during the recording of the show? Simple.

BAN BOOZE!

Seriously, that's what they did. They banned alcohol and put everybody in theatre-like seats instead of the usually boozy tables. Rather than the very cool music awards it should be, it ended up looking like the Oscars. That's not what you want from the Brits, a load of people sitting uncomfortably in small seats. Personally I rather enjoyed some of the carnage. You don't get much carnage from Busted being sat down behind Tom Jones!

This was also when I first noticed something that was to be repeated in future years. Radio 1 has always had a decent involvement in the Brits. Most years our listeners are asked to vote for the Best British Breakthrough Artist. What exactly they're breaking through I've no idea, but this year the award went to Mr Will Young. All week on the radio I'd been asking my audience to vote for Will. I'd met him a few times and really liked him. I also thought he had done very well, turning himself from an average guy on a reality television show called *Pop Idol* into actually a very successful recording artist. My audience voted and Will won. I was really pleased for him when they called his name out, but a few seconds later, I was swearing under my breath. He thanked his record company, he thanked his producers and he thanked his management team. In fact, the only people he didn't thank were the Radio 1 listeners who voted for him.

Silly boy. The next day we spent a good hour goofing on him until he popped a card round apologising and saying that of course he wanted to thank the listeners. I let him off.

Davina McCall hosted that year and was brilliant, but without any alcohol, the awards were ever so slightly lacklustre, so twelve months later, guess what? The booze returned. Hurray!

I'd started presenting the breakfast show on Radio 1 in 2004 so I was honoured when I was asked to give out an award. This was very exciting. I was working backstage recording interviews for the radio show until my call time came and I was ushered into a waiting room at the side of the stage, ready to go and give out the award for the Best British Breakthrough Act. And the winner was: Busted. And once again in the great tradition of these 'voted for by the Radio 1 listeners awards', Busted didn't thank the Radio 1 listeners. They broke up shortly after.

In 2005 me and the radio team were once again working backstage recording interviews with the nominees and winners. After each interview we posed for a Polaroid photo, which I was told we would give away on the radio the next day. I remember thinking it was a slightly odd prize, a photo of me with somebody famous, but I went with it. It turned out that the cheeky monkeys on my team had planned to take lots of photos and then put them in a frame and present it to me for my birthday the following week. In all the years I have done radio, and of all the hundreds of interviews I have done, I don't actually have many photos of the people I've met. I don't care if this sounds sad, but to me this was a really lovely present, a snapshot of my life for one night in 2005. It hangs proudly on my wall at home. There's me and Robbie Williams, me and Sharon Osbourne, Green Day, Gwen Stefani, Muse, Joss Stone, Keane, Franz Ferdinand, Will Young and, best of all, my little *Chris Moyles Show* team slap bang in the middle. See, I'm not always an egotistical bighead. I can be an emotional boy sometimes – as long as it's all to do with me, obviously.

Just before the 2006 awards, Chris Martin from Coldplay appeared on our show. I love the band and was excited to interview him, and as usual we began the interview by playing an audio biography of him. These are always written by Comedy Dave and voiced by Aled. They are deliberately wrong and they make me laugh every time we play them. They take the piss out of our guest before they've even entered the studio. This is what Dave wrote about Chris Martin and it was played just before he walked in.

> Chris Martin was born in England years ago and is the pianist and lead singer in the band Coldplay along with three other blokes, although nobody knows what they're called. Coldplay was discovered by Steve Lamacq, who promised to make them all stars. Sadly Steve couldn't work his magic on all the band, but he did manage to make Chris Martin famous and this is how he managed to score himself a celebrity wife in the form of Gweenyth Paltry.

> A man of strong morals and values, Chris Martin is aiming to save the world, free Nelson Mandela and end poverty and stuff along with other famous types like Bono, Brandon Block, Sting and Apache Indian. They plan to make poor people history and through awareness and gigs and the like they should be able to

do it. Apparently Live Aid was his idea and Bob Gandolf and Midge Ure regard him as an inspirationalist even though he confesses to being a bit forgetful. Which is why he has to write everything down on his hands.

'Some people have Filofaxes but I just use my hands,' says Chris. And it's wise words like that that have made him one of the most important people in world history.

Chris hadn't slept that night and immediately the interview entered the world of surreal.

Chris: *I just got back from America and I'm so happy to be home that I haven't been to sleep.*

Me: *How long have you been away for?*

Chris: *Twelve years. We did a gig last night in Abbey Road then I went home and had hot dogs, but not real dogs of course.*

Dave: *You mean like sausages?*

Chris: *They were like fake sausages. Fosauges.*

Me: *Right, is that what they're called?*

Chris: *That's what I'm calling them and if I say jump you say, 'How high?'*

Me: *OK say it.*

Chris: *Fosauges*

Me: *How high?*

As I said, it was surreal. Later in the interview, I started taking the piss out of his appearance. As I said, he hadn't slept and his hair was all over the place. Honestly, the guy looked like he'd been dragged through a hedge.

Me: *So is the crazy hair staying for tomorrow night?*

Chris: *Listen, this is a look. This is not crazy.*

Me: *It's a look that only you have.*

Chris: *It's because I'm doing Michael Bolton on* Stars in Their Eyes *on Saturday.*

Me: *I tell you what, if you can get a bit of 'How can we be lovers if we can't be friends' into your set at the Brits tomorrow, then I will give ten pounds to charity.*

Chris: *Will you give it to the charity for us to stop poor people?*

Me: *Yeah, in fact, here's the deal, if you sing a bit of Michael Bolton tomorrow night at the Brits, I will promise to be nice to a poor person.*

Chris: *(Laughing) You're a bastard!*

It was a great interview and Chris left happy. The next night at the Brits, we were working in our backstage studio when the guy from Chris Martin's record company burst through the door.

'Please tell me you heard that.'

'Heard what?' I asked.

It turned out that halfway through Coldplay's performance of 'Square One', Chris grabbed the microphone and sang 'How can we be lovers if we can't be friends'.

It remains one of my most surreal yet proudest moments. There's also the time I autographed Joss Stone's leg with a permanent marker pen, and if you don't believe me, the bloody picture is in the photo section. I love the Brits!

TECHNOLOGY
GEEK

I find as I get older that I get more into 'bits'. You know, gadgets and stuff. Sure, when I was a kid I liked these bits but now I seem to have a very unhealthy love of them, and I convince myself they are not just toys, but essential items for my day-to-day life. It also never seems to end, with new and improved machines being thought up that I just have to buy.

First up are those clever little devices to listen to music on, and I LOVE music. People are surprised when I say that because they hear the radio show and think I'm not interested in it. How can you not love music? Just because I don't have a record of the week or rave on and on about this new cool band doesn't mean I don't listen to music all day, every day. I can't live without it. To be in the *Big Brother* house would kill me if I couldn't listen to some kind of music. Don't get me wrong. I don't like everything. In fact, people who listen to and enjoy Country and Western music should be rounded up and sent to live in the Falkland Islands for their own good and the good of the rest of us.

So in the beginning there were Walkmans. I don't think I ever had a 'proper' Walkman, but I did have a cheaper alternative. It was great, stick your cassettes in – in my case it was *The Hits Album* – and away you went. I don't know if you remember *The Hits Album* but it was like a rival to the *Now That's What I Call Music* compilations. It was a double cassette that featured the hits of the day, such as Prince, Michael Jackson, Howard Jones and Wham. It was great. I listened to it so much that I knew what track was next without even looking at the inlay sleeve. Fast forward a few years and the Discman came out. This time it played not cassettes but CDs. Amazing. Again, we couldn't afford the sexy original machines, so a cheaper alternative would arrive at Christmas. Santa really was a cheap bastard to my brother and me when we were growing up. I don't know if he used to get these off Big John in the pub or what. Anyway, you'd stick your CD in the machine, pop your headphones on and away you went. Portable CD music. The only problem being that it took about a thousand batteries to run the thing and it was like walking around with a massive compact, like girls use to hide their spots.

Fast forward into the new millennium and something came along called an iPod. Now this, I didn't get. I remember when they came out thinking it was a pointless device.

> *So, you buy your CD. Then you buy the iPod. You load the iPod software on to your computer. Then you import the CD into your iTunes library. Then you get a wire or two and connect the iPod to your computer and then download the CD you have just imported to your computer library on to your iPod. What is the point of that? You may as well dig out your old Discman, stick the bloody CD in it and off you go!*

Now, of course, I am almost obsessive about it. I love the technology and buy and download music from the internet almost daily. And this is where the trouble begins.

So I have an iPod, which means I have to buy every single accessory that comes with it. When you open the box you get some nice little headphones. They work fine and sound great, until a friend tells me about 'noise-reduction headphones'. Now they sound sexy. So I get a pair. (Actually Sophie bought me a pair for Christmas.) You stick them on and flick the special switch, and the cushion gets vacuumed round your ear and keeps the noise of the outside world away from your music and your delicate little ears. I LOVE THEM. If you ever use a pair on a plane, close your eyes and you really forget where you are. The only problem with the headphones is that they are quite large and make you look like Craig David from *Bo' Selecta!*

So I have the iPod and I have the cool headphones, but I like to listen to it at home and the headphones are just not practical. So I begin searching, and I find that some clever people have designed a big speaker that you plug your iPod into, and you can listen to it as loud as you want, in brilliant quality. I gotta get me one of these bad boys. And so I do.

I can now listen to my music on my great headphones and I can now listen to my music at home on my big speaker. But what if I am in the car? Simple. These clever people have thought of everything. It's a device you stick into your iPod and it broadcasts your music on a tiny FM frequency. Tune your radio into it and you have 'iPod FM' playing all your favourite tunes. Jesus I love technology.

But where does it all stop?

In the old days mobile phones were the size of a small fat child and had to be carried around on a trolley. (Probably quite similar to some fat children!) It really does make you feel old when you remember a time when mobile phones were only for yuppies. When you had to find a phone box to make a call, only to realise that most of them were either smashed up or stank of piss. I was in my twenties by the time I got my first mobile and looking back I have no idea how I survived without it.

It was like a brick and had a little flap to guard the keypad and an aerial you had to pull out in order to get a better signal. There was only a tiny screen and that was to see what number you were punching in. Cameras on a phone were a thing of dreams back then. As time went by and technology improved, the phones got smaller and more advanced. These days you can access the internet from your phone. You can record video and send it to your home computer. You can get sat nav on it and you can play music while checking your emails. All of this is brilliant. However, all I want the bloody thing to do is to make and receive phone calls, text my mates and maybe take some pictures or video. I don't need most of the stuff my phone will do. What I get really fed up with is predictive texting.

Hey pal. Fancy the sub tonight. He so let of know.

What the hell's that? I know what I meant to say, and it didn't feature a 'sub'.

I just got a new phone and Aled has been swapping all the information from my old phone on to my new one. I didn't even know you could do this, so I watched in amazement as he got the two phones 'talking' to each other. I must admit I couldn't hear them though.

I haven't been able to text anybody for the past few days and it has been so annoying. However, I have been calling people back straight away instead. It's made me realise that I don't speak to people enough. Most of the people who text me were shocked when I called them.

'Oh my God, you've called me. Are you all right?'

How rude?

I recently bought a new car and decided I would get a few toys for that as well. My friend got a car with a TV built into it and I was very impressed. We were sitting in his car in the driveway watching Sky Sports News, and then E4 and then E4+1. How cool was that? I mean sure we could've gone inside the house and watched the exact same channels on a huge widescreen TV, but that's not the point. It was clever technology. We were watching TV in my mate's car. Brilliant. So I decided I was going to get a TV built into my car too. It doesn't work while you are moving, but it does work while you are stationary. This is a safety feature to prevent morons crashing into other cars while they are watching *Loose Women* instead of watching the road. I reckoned I spent enough time not moving, stuck in traffic on the M1, to justify getting it.

Press a button in the car and the TV screen lifts up to reveal a memory card slot. Much as I love the technology, I'm not sure what the hell it does. My friend Simon assured me that the memory card thing was very useful. Simply load up your memory card with all your favourite songs in an MP3 format (still with me?) and bingo: you've got thousands of songs at the touch of a button without having to drag your iPod or a pile of CDs along with you. Brilliant. The only trouble is I have no idea how to do it and it still has just the tracks my friend put on there as an example – and there is only so much Gilbert O'Sullivan I can handle!

The next thing I'm obsessed about doing is hiding my wires. That's not a euphemism, Mrs: I mean exactly what I say. At home I have a Big TV. I also have a Skybox, a DVD player, a video, an Xbox and a mini disc recorder, which I use to record clips for work. Add to that the surround sound system, which I've also never really figured out but it sounds good enough to me. All these machines either have wires coming out all over the place or a bloody remote control. My living room is like a social club for remote controls. I currently have seven, all of which drive Sophie mad. When she tries to watch TV, the stereo comes on instead. And don't even get me started on when the batteries run out. One of the remotes is so difficult to get the back off I swear the manufacturers glued the bloody thing down. In fact, there is a rumour that George Clooney is going to make *Ocean's 14* all about trying to break into my remote.

Sophie's uncle Trevor has the wires for his surround hidden inside the walls. Now that is cool. I have my wires sellotaped down the wall and across the doors to the conservatory and down to the TV. Not so cool. So wireless is the way forward. My Xbox has a wireless controller. It also has a wireless headset. (Don't ask, it's geeky.) So why can't I have a wireless TV? Why can't they invent a wireless TV you don't even need a remote for? Simply shout the name of the show you want to watch, and on it comes. Although that would mean Sophie finding out that I secretly like to watch *Heartbeat* on a Sunday night.

Sophie has recently got caught up in my technology obsession. I came home the other day and she told me that there was a voicemail message from a guy about something I'd ordered from the internet.

Oh Jesus, I've been caught out, I thought. I can't believe that Sophie's going to find out that I've secretly been ordering … hang on. Ordering what? I can't remember ordering anything off the internet.

'The message said that it wasn't released yet and did you still want to buy it.'

Buy it? Buy what exactly? I couldn't remember ordering anything from … oh no. Shit. I do remember something.

A few weeks before, my friend Asa and I had been talking about a little gadget that was going to be released later in the year. Now strap yourselves in because this is quite nerdy.

It's an R2-D2 projector.

I know, I'm very sorry.

Basically this thing is a replica of R2-D2 from the *Star Wars* movies. It moves around just like the real thing (I know the real thing isn't actually real) and even makes lots of R2 beeps and sounds. But the cool thing is you stick a DVD into it and it projects the image from its robot head on to a wall. Cool, isn't it? It also has an iPod connector and a bloody memory card slot as well. So you can play your music and have him follow you round from room to room. And if you're reading this and you're into *Star Wars* and you're thinking, Chris, I actually like the sound of this, well let me tell you that the remote control looks like the Millennium Falcon! I'm exhausted just thinking about it.

Anyway, Asa and I were talking about it one day, and the next thing I know he's gone and ordered one. These things are limited edition and I didn't want to be left out. So I headed home after the pub one night and decided to log on to the internet and get one for myself. The only thing was, I couldn't really remember doing it.

Technology gets me into trouble. If it's not ordering bizarre geeky things off the internet, it's confusing my girlfriend as to which remote control actually controls what.

Or it's annoying my girlfriend by having a flat full of crap I never use.

'How come you keep all the boxes for what you buy?' she'll ask.

'Because if I ever need to take it back, I'll still have the box for it,' I say, knowing full well I'm talking rubbish. I'm a hoarder. I can't help it. I also have a spare room that doubles as an office and a place for me to keep all the crap I can't yet throw away. It's not my fault. Sure I buy some weird things, but I also get given a lot of stuff. Some of this stuff is brilliant, and some of it is rubbish. For my birthday recently, I was sent a replica of a Lightsabre from *Star Wars*. Now this thing is cool. It lights up and even makes all the noises. When I was a kid I had a plastic Lightsabre that was basically a torch with a red tube. This thing actually looks real. It's brilliant and you can't help but wave it around and pretend you're a Jedi. Yes I know … but I challenge any *Star Wars* fan, male or female, to not have a little go on it. Even Sophie has had a few moments of waving it around the flat making the Lightsabre noise. Now bear in mind that for the same birthday I got a Spam Hat. It's a foam hat that looks like a tin of Spam. I can't throw that away because it was a present from Sophie. In the same way that I can't yet throw away what the rest of my radio team bought me for my birthday.

Carrie got me a plug-in lava lamp. It's a mini lava lamp that plugs into your laptop. What the fuck do I want one of them for? But I don't say that, obviously, because it's a present and I don't want to seem rude. I also got a karate fighter desktop arcade game. Again, why do I need this? But Carrie isn't alone. Comedy Dave bought me Spy Glass. These are sunglasses with built-in headphones and a microphone so you can secretly chat with your friend who's wearing the other pair. Oh yeah: I've got a pair of the things. Dominic bought me some night-vision goggles with a sonic ear device. The idea is that you wear these at night and can see in the dark. You can also hear the slightest movement or sound.

WHO DO THESE PEOPLE THINK I AM?

They must see me as a part-time spy, part-time bored person, who will enjoy watching their mini lava lamp during breaks playing on my karate fighter desktop arcade game. I am neither and I don't.

But what can I tell you? I'm a technology geek and I love it. I love bits and fancy gadgets and things that beep or light up. I like cool speakers and wireless things. I know it's not just me, and I also know I'm not the worst.

My friend Simon has a radio studio in his spare bedroom. And I don't mean a CD player and a microphone. He's got a proper working radio studio upstairs in his house. Jingle machines, record decks, the works. To make it worse, the guy is actually employed as a DJ. He works on the radio in real life.

So he broadcasts from his house then, Chris? you're thinking to yourself. *That's quite clever.*

NO! He doesn't. He has to drive thirty minutes to work every day and he's not allowed to broadcast from his home studio.

And in his proper bedroom, not only does he have speakers for his surround sound hidden in his walls, he also has a bloody speaker under the floorboards beneath his bed.

In his garage he has the actual record players from the old BBC Radio 2 studios that are so heavy and big he doesn't know what to do with them.

And to cap it all off, he bids for old copies of the *Radio Times* on eBay.

I must say that I do love Simon, though. Apart from anything else, he makes me feel less geeky!

GUEST DIARY BITS:
Part 2

29 January
RICKY WILSON – KAISER CHIEFS

I LOVE this band. Not only are they from Leeds, but they are also bloody good. Ricky came in and the interview was going OK, that was until Ricky's phone went off and he decided to read the text live on air. That was the moment that he, and the rest of our millions of listeners, found out that Ricky was going to be an uncle. Bless him.

RATING: 42.06 OUT OF 60

1 February
KELLY OSBOURNE

I've met her lots of times and for some reason I like her. I say
for some reason because she can be a spoilt little brat, moody
and generally a pain in the arse. But she is also very sweet
and makes me laugh. Every time she comes on the show I flirt
with her and tell her how we should go out with each other. She
just gets embarrassed and tells me to stop. I'd like to think
that it's because she secretly likes me, but I think it's actually
because she finds me repulsive!

RATING: 47.43 OUT OF 60

22 February
JOSS STONE

Oh dear. What can I say?

When I first met Joss, when her debut single was released, she
was a sweet innocent little girl Then she went to America and
came back a bit of an arse. She appeared at the Brits wearing
a very colourful dress. Joss reminded me during the interview
that I had said she looked like a hooker that had fallen into a

vat of Smarties'. Anyway, she came on to present an award and pranced around the stage talking with an American accent. It all went horribly wrong, and the crowd, and seemingly most of the country, turned against her. So the record company asked if she could come on the show and explain herself. I knew I was the man to tell her what had gone wrong.

Despite the fact that she pissed off a lot of the audience with her naivety, I think it was one of the most compelling interviews we have ever done. I have to explain that she is very young and just hasn't experienced life enough to be able to deal with it better. She has spent a lot of time in the States and that has really affected her. Nobody in Britain likes anybody who appears to be pretending to be something they're not. I don't think she is pretending, I just think she doesn't know who she is yet. Also nobody likes a moaner and Joss seemed to come across as just that.

We were talking about her bizarre transatlantic accent when I said: 'You need to hang out with Robbie Williams, then you'll come back with a Stoke accent.'

'I don't have time to hang out with anybody. Not even my dogs.'

'Yes, you do. You do have time,' I said. 'If I have time to hang out with dogs than so have you.'

'Yeah, but you're not flying around the world every three minutes.'

'Oh, see, nobody will feel sorry for you if you say that. People would love to fly around the world.'

I tried to explain to her that flying first class around the world may indeed be tiring, but you've got to keep that information to yourself, and when somebody asks how you are, instead of saying, 'I'm tired because I'm flying around the world first class,' you should just say, 'I'm great thanks. A bit tired but I'm great.'

I DO like her though. I think she is sweet and a genuinely nice girl, but sadly she spent too much time in America and it makes her come across as fake. It wouldn't surprise me if she turned out to be the next Whitney Houston. But let's hope it's without a marriage to Bobby Brown and a penchant for chemicals.

RATING: 27.2 OUT OF 60

28 February
JONATHAN ROSS

He came into the studio to talk about Comic Relief and Red Nose Day and we were all pleased to have him on the show. I've been a fan of his since I first saw him hosting his TV show 'The Last Resort'. I even saw him make a very early appearance with David Letterman while I was on holiday in America when I was sixteen. Previously my meetings with Jonathan hadn't gone that well and I had always thought he didn't like me. But after the interview with him I started to believe that maybe he doesn't mind me after all. I hope so because I think we have a lot in common. We are both great broadcasters and extremely good-looking with it! So let's hope he likes me. I mean, I don't know if he'll invite me round to his house for a game of tennis, but you never know. Actually, I'd rather have a beer with him, as I'm shite at tennis.

RATING: 46.845 OUT OF 60

20 March
THE PROCLAIMERS

I'm going to let you into a secret. It's such a secret that I'm not sure if Comedy Dave or Dominic and Carrie even know about this. Occasionally, we'll have some guests on the show, and I'm not entirely sure of their names. Obviously I don't mean that I forget them, but I mean that sometimes I get mixed up as to which one is which. I've been like that ever since I interviewed the pop band 911. Any one of them could've been called Spike because none of them had spiky hair. So fast-forward to one morning on Radio 1 when the Proclaimers came in to promote their new record. I didn't know which one was which and even after I got introduced to them I knew that I would panic and forget. So what I do is simple but very effective. I write their names down on the top of my notes and have an arrow pointing to the side of the radio desk they are sitting. Brilliant, hey? So for the whole interview I got to call them by their correct names. That is, if they were sitting in the right place. If they had moved I might not have noticed and that could've been embarrassing.

'So, Charlie, tell me about the single.'

'I'm over here, Chris!'

Anyway I have liked the band for years and was honoured when they played an acoustic version of a couple of their songs for us.

RATING: Not sure if we rated them so I'll give them 35 OUT OF 60

28 March
DAVID TENNANT

You often hear about 'how nice' certain famous people are. Well, let me confirm that David Tennant is a nice guy. It was his first time on the show but we had met before so it was nice to see him again. As a huge fan of 'Doctor Who', it should have been weird talking to him because he's different to his on-screen persona. For a start he's not a Time Lord, travelling around the universe saving people from aliens and stuff whilst Billie Piper, or whoever it is, follows him around. And secondly, he's Scottish and doesn't sound anything like Doctor Who. He is, though, very nice and, so it seems, very popular. When he was on the show we got loads of texts from listeners who just seemed to love him! He's popular and nice, and seemingly very down to earth, if you'll pardon the pun. As you know we rate our guests, but with David we thought he should rate us too. He rated us 48.5 out of 60. Just ever so slightly higher than we rated him!

RATING: 45.732 OUT OF 60

27 November
PHILIP GLENISTER

I LOVED 'Life on Mars', the fantastic BBC series about a policeman who ends up in a coma and seemingly wakes up in the past. Philip Glenister played the brilliant DCI Hunt, and when he came on the show he was surprisingly posher in real life. I know how television works but sometimes somebody is SO good, that you forget they're acting. However, when he poses for a photo and puts his scary policeman face on, you actually believe that you're being arrested!

RATING: 38.02 OUT OF 60 (should've been more)

30 April
NATASHA BEDINGFIELD

If it wasn't for the fact that it would mean Daniel Bedingfield would be my brother-in-law, I would contemplate marrying Natasha Bedingfield. If it wasn't for the fact that I am overweight and funny looking, I am sure she would marry me too.

RATING: 39.95 OUT OF 60

11 May
DAVID GEST

OK, so for those of you who don't know about this already, David Gest was married to Liza Minnelli. Then he went into the jungle on 'I'm A Celebrity, Get Me Out Of Here!' Next ITV gave him his own fly-on-the-wall documentary and he was booked on the show to talk about that and another show he was doing, 'Grease Is The Word'. However, we received a text message from his PR person saying they would be five minutes late. We called them back to try and find out where they were. The text was timed at 8.15am, and by 8.30 there was no sign of him. I lost my temper and it kicked off!

'Where the hell is my guest David Gest?' I screamed at Aled.

'He is still on his way. I have spoken to his people,' replied Aled.

'And how far away are they?'

'About a mile.'

'Right, if he's not here by the end of the news and sport then he's off the show, guest or no guest.'

Dominic read the news and Carrie read the sport, and he still wasn't in the building.

'That's the end of the news and sport then. Right, Rachel, talk to me. Is David Gest in the building?' I looked at Rachel and she looked at Aled.

'I need a Yes or No. Aled?' Aled looked at Rachel.

'Right, finished, he's out. David Gest is cancelled this morning.'

It had finally happened, we had cancelled our first-ever guest, live on the air. I've a funny feeling it isn't the last time this will happen.

RATING: 0 OUT OF 60

25 May
OZZY AND SHARON OSBOURNE

We had only expected Ozzy but then Sharon turned up as well. We spoke to the Prince of Darkness first and Dave got the interview off to a great start by telling him that he smelt nice. Who the hell tells Ozzy Osbourne that he smells nice? He had just flown in from LA and began to tell us about his house.

'They have these tours of famous people's places, "here is the home of whoever", you know, and people think that they can just walk around.'

'Ozzy, I've been on one of those tours,' I admitted.

'You have? You lemon.'

He was on great form and so very funny. He really is a funny man. Then Sharon came and joined in. She called Robbie Williams 'miserable' because he never came round for cuddles any more. Ozzy piped up:

'Is that one of our dogs?'

'Cuddles?' asked Sharon. 'No, don't be silly.'

We then joked about Louis Walsh being fired from 'The X Factor'.

'Poor old Louis, God rest his soul' I joked.

'Has he died?' asked Ozzy.

'NO!' screamed Sharon. 'Don't listen to Chris.'

It was a brilliant morning, so much fun sitting there and watching the pair of them.

RATING: 57.58 OUT OF 60

6 July
DAVE GROHL

Foo Fighters frontman Dave Grohl came on the show and not only watched in awe as Dominic and Dave's folk band, Folk Face, played him a special song about the environment, but he also played Dom's guitar and gave us a sneak preview of the Foos' new album. He looked like Jesus with his big beard, but didn't sound like him because Jesus wasn't from Ohio. We asked our guest if he would like to rate us. And I got eleven out of ten. He called me The President of English Morning Radio, which was very nice of him. So thank you Dave, you bloody kiss arse!

RATING: 53.02 OUT OF 60

13
KEEPING IT REAL

When, at the age of eighteen, I went off to Luxembourg to make a name for myself in radio, little did I know that for a while I'd be doing exactly that. I had to change my name because the station had hired a DJ with a similar surname to mine, and as I was the youngest DJ there, it was decided that I would change my name. I wanted to keep Chris so I chose Holmes as my surname, as it was my mum's maiden name. So there I was, Chris Moyles, talking on the radio as Chris Holmes. It was weird because I felt like I was pretending to be somebody else. I had jingles that said 'Chris Holmes' but I never liked playing them because it felt like I was playing them for somebody else, as if I was pushing the buttons for a DJ who was sitting in another room.

I always wanted to be Chris Moyles on the radio because it's who I am. Especially now when the show is the most honest it's ever been. I don't know how these DJs live with the fact that they're called one thing at home, and another thing when they go to work. It's almost like they are living a double life. And maybe some of them are. Maybe they leave their wife and kids at home and then arrive at work with a totally new identity. It would be a way of having two women on the go, I suppose, but then how many men can cope with one woman, let alone two? Surely that's just double the headache.

[Note to any lazy book reviewers who hate my guts: you can use that in your review about how sexist I am. Keep a lookout for a few more quotes to back up your predictable rubbish review. I'll try and tick all your obvious boxes by the time we reach the end of the book. It'll be like 'stereotype lazy journalist bingo'!]

I had to change my name, I had no choice. As soon as the job finished and I headed back to England, I became Chris Moyles again, and not a moment too soon. But there are DJs on the radio who have chosen to change their name themselves. They haven't been pressured and don't even have a horrible real name, it's just that for some bizarre reason they think a new name will sound better. More DJ like. This is a thought that only a DJ could come up with. Because as I have said before:

ALL DJS ARE STUPID

Almost without comparison, they are a gaggle of morons. They have bad hair, bad clothes and bad personal hygiene. Yes, they know a lot about music, but it's always chart music. They have spent so long playing the Top Ten at Ten that they can pretty much quote you the entire *Guinness Book of Hit Singles* from cover to cover. Trust me, all DJs are dumb.

'But, Chris,' you may ask me, 'what about your friends on Radio 1?'

'What about them?' I reply.

'The DJs on the station you actually like. Those we the audience

like. Are you saying that Jo Whiley has bad personal hygiene and bad clothes?'

Well, she certainly doesn't have bad personal hygiene, but the clothes are debatable. (That was a joke, Jo!)

OK, I'll admit, NOT EVERY SINGLE DJ in the world is dumb, there are always exceptions to the rule, but if you picked 100 of them at random, you would find that 97 of them were exactly as I have described. No skills in dealing with members of the opposite sex. No skills in dealing with confrontation. No skills such as cooking or DIY. And they always love shite music. That's a guarantee. No matter what age they are they will almost certainly have an unhealthy obsession with Cat Stevens. Or ELO. Or Supertramp. TRUST ME, IT'S THE LAW.

It's just one of those stereotypes that happens to be true. There are others, such as footballers. All footballers have lots of money and no taste or original thought. I know a few footballers, in fact one of my best friends is a professional footballer, and chances are that he would back me up. One of the things I have noticed about footballers is their habit of copying other footballers but trying to better them. If one of the boys buys a big house in a certain area, another footballer will buy a slightly bigger house in the same area. If one of them buys a flash expensive watch that is actually disgusting, then another footballer will buy a watch from the same disgusting range, but one that is ever so slightly more expensive. If one of them buys a car, then another footballer will buy a similar car. Almost the same, but slightly different.

I recently went to the Tottenham Hotspur training ground with a competition winner from our Comic Relief week. One of the prizes was to train with my friend Paul Robinson, the Spurs and England goalkeeper. The first thing you notice in the players' car park is that every car is black. And I mean, EVERY SINGLE ONE. They are all different, no two cars are the same, except they are ALL black. Not one blue car or one red car. All of them are black. Why? Because they are footballers, and this is what they do. Once upon a time, somebody somewhere said to a footballer:

'You should get that new car in black, mate. It'll look nicer.'

And the rest is history. Because one person said it, it's fact, and all other footballers must follow suit. They're like sheep, but with more expensive horrible watches.

Glamour models are the same when it comes to stereotype. Now, most men love a glamour model. They're pretty, sexy, but generally thick as shit. Yeah yeah, somebody reading this will be thinking:

'But that's not true, Chris. My mate Kylie is a glamour model and she's not stupid.'

Well, I'm afraid I have two pieces of bad news for you. One, your friend Kylie is thick as shit, and two, you probably are too. Sorry, love, it's not my fault, I don't make the rules. It's just that stereotypes are often true. Glamour models are stupid like footballers are too rich with bad taste. In the same way that supply teachers at school were very nice people who weren't cut out to be proper teachers. They didn't have what it took to take control of a class and impose order. Which is why whenever you had a supply teacher come into your class, you knew it was 'do whatever you want' time.

Footballers, glamour models, supply teachers and DJs. They all conform to type, just like all fat girls love cake!

But back to what I was saying. DJs often think they should change their name when they get on the radio. Top choice is to give themselves two first names. It's easy and anybody can do it. You keep your first name and then you choose a surname that is just your average Christian name and add an 's' to it (unless it already ends in 's', in which case you don't even have to do that). Tune round the radio dial and you will surely come across examples of this.

Mike Johns

Dave Peters

Steve Simons

Pete James

Andi Peters

Oops. Sorry, Andi!

I don't know why they do it but they do, and in their hundreds.

The second option is to come up with a wacky made-up name. In Ireland there was a radio station based just outside Dublin called Atlantic 252. When they launched, and for a good few years after, almost all of their DJs had silly made-up names. They either landed at the radio station with a name already, such as Charlie Wolf or Dusty Rhodes, or they were given one, such as:

Rick O'Shea

Cliff Walker

Robin Banks

Who thinks these names up?! Even one of my best friends has a ridiculous name, Sandy Beech. Yes, I have a friend called Sandy Beech. I have known him since we were kids at Radio Aire in Leeds and now he runs a brilliant music production company called Music 4. Together we make the jingles for my show. When I say we make them together, I mean that I write the words and he does EVERY-THING ELSE. The rest of the radio team have know him for years too, but it was only after about five years of knowing him that Aled realised that 'Sandy Beech' sounded made-up. Bless him. Sandy is also good friends with Dusty Rhodes. Can you imagine making those two plane reservations? Add Bam Bam to our collective list of friends and now it looks like I'm the outsider because I'm called Chris Moyles.

So I kept my real name and I think it was the right thing to do. Occasionally a situation will arise where I wish that I HAD changed my name to something else. Like the time when Dave and I were involved in a car crash. I say a car crash: some guy flew through the traffic lights and sent us spinning in the middle of the road. The side of my car was smashed in and the car that hit us looked like the engine was now in the back seat. Luckily we were all OK but we were in shock. I remember feeling fine and then looking down at my hands to see that they were shaking uncontrollably. Dave wanted to sit down and compose himself. I'd never been in an accident like this before so I sat with him for a while and we both just caught our breath. Then we walked to Dave's house, which was nearby, and by the time we got there we had both calmed down a bit. We had a nice strong cup of tea, which, as my mother will tell you, is the solution to almost anything, and then I called the insurance people to inform them of the accident.

'And what name is it, love?' said the bored woman on the phone.

'It's Moyles. M O Y L E S.'

'And your first name, love?' she continued, bored out of her mind.

'It's Chris.'

'Chris Moyles?' She perked up.

'Yeah, that's right.'

'Oh My God. Really? I can't believe it. Chris Moyles the DJ? Wow, Chris Moyles.' Now she was awake. 'Chris Moyles, how exciting.' Then all of a sudden her tone changed. 'Hang on. Am I on the radio right now?'

'No, you're not,' I assured her.

'I am, aren't I? I'm live on the radio right now. Is this one of them wind-ups? It is, isn't it? I'm being wound up, aren't I?'

'No, love, I can assure you you're not being wound up,' I said, amazed.

'Are you sure?' she cackled. 'Are you sure I'm not on the radio right now?'

I snapped. 'Yes, I'm sure you're not on the radio right now. Because I myself am not on the radio right now. In fact, I'm only talking to you *BECAUSE I'VE JUST HAD A FUCKING CAR CRASH!'*

Dave looked at up at me. The phone went silent for about two seconds, until I heard, 'Are you sure?'

Looking like twats for charity.

Me and Dave.

Me and Dad.

Me and Kelly Osbourne.

Me and the best team in radio
(oh, and Richard our jingle singer).

With Matt Lucas as Marjorie Dawes.

Joss Stone as a tube of smarties!

Me signing her leg in permanent ink.

A few of my guests ...

Keith Allen

Will Ferrell

Take That

James Nesbitt

Lily Allen

Russell Brand

David Beckham

Ozzy and Sharon Osbourne

© BBC

Philip Glenister

David Tennant

© BBC

Richy Wilson

© BBC

The Proclaimers

Dave Grohl

© BBC

Hello Wembley!

It's a small price to pay for keeping my real name and my real identity. The idea of saying something like this on the radio every morning:

'Good morning, everybody, this is Tarzan Moyles here on Radio 1!'

really doesn't appeal. And sure, occasionally I will get grief because I am known by my real name, but at least I don't get grief AND have a silly made-up name. That must be even worse. In fact, I was having this conversation only last night with my good friend Mike Hunt. You wouldn't believe the problems this boy has!

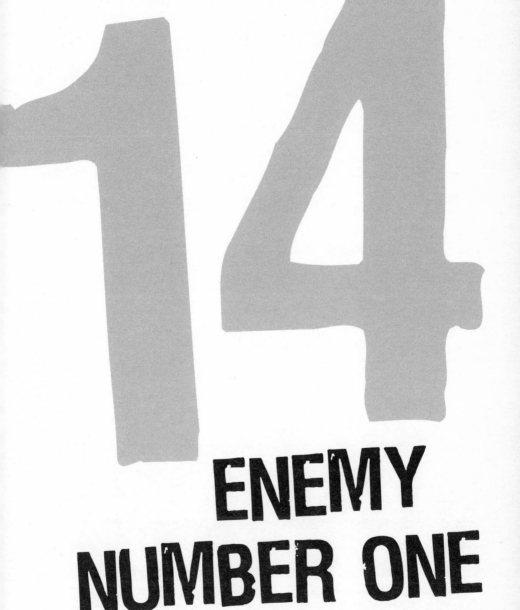

14

ENEMY NUMBER ONE

I'm on the radio every weekday morning for three hours a day. For those of you who listen regularly, you may possibly be aware that we don't play as much music as most other breakfast radio shows. In fact, the top pain-in-the-ass moan I have to deal with at work is being asked if I could play more music. And I try, I really do. I know it's not a talk show and I don't want it to be. I love being on Radio 1 and playing the music we play, but the truth is that sometimes records get dropped because a guest is very funny, or a throwaway bit just keeps going and it's just too good to stop halfway through to play the new Justin Timberlake. Luckily the audience figures show that the listeners love all the 'banter' and that saves my ass, but it's hard sometimes because the station needs to play certain records a certain number of times, and I'm not really helping. This is a problem I am aware of. I understand it, and as I said, I try to do something about it. When you're on the radio for fifteen hours a week, that's a lot of material you have to come up with. And I'm lucky that I have the BEST team working on the show. Rachel and Aled work very hard at coming up with features and bits for me to goof on. Dave is great with competitions and song parodies. Dominic is brilliant at thinking of ideas during the show and then going off and recording and editing it so we can play it the same morning. And Carrie, well, God love her, she does stuff as well! The point is, we all work hard at making fifteen hours of funny radio every week.

However, you can't please everybody all the time. And at the same time, what is funny to one thousand people might not be funny to one person. Someone might even be offended at what I've said or joked about. I don't want to offend anybody; I just want to make people laugh first thing in the morning.

AND THIS IS AN ONGOING BATTLE, EVERY SINGLE DAY.

I've been on the radio for a long time. I like to think that we all talk like everybody else talks. We chat about what you might chat about at work. We watch the same TV shows that you watch. We talk about normal things because we're normal people. Granted we have a slightly abnormal job, sitting in a room broadcasting a conversation that is heard by millions of people, but we're all the same. During my time working on the radio I've found out things you can say and things you can't. And it's interesting to discover which subjects attract complaints, and which don't.

For example, make a joke about a cute animal, and the pet lovers of the UK will be on the phone or text immediately. I'm a meat-eater; I love chicken, pork, beef and lamb. I just love meat, and I don't have any pets either.

I can't really have pets, because I can't trust myself that I won't be looking at the dog thinking: Mmm, I wonder what he'd taste like, slightly barbecued with a side of relish.

If I were to say that on the radio at 8.15 one morning, I would get an extraordinary number of complaints.

However, say anything about French people, and I mean ANYTHING, and we won't hear a thing. Nothing. I know this because I've done both and been surprised by the reaction. For whatever reason, people don't mind a joke about the French – but don't you dare say anything about their dog. Mix the two together:

> Well, he's French, he's probably looking at the dog thinking: That would look good in a baguette …

and we will receive NO complaints, because I'm talking about a French person. Ridiculous, isn't it? But it's true.

I really don't want to offend anybody. But sometimes I do. So if you don't mean to cause offence but you still do, what then? Can somebody be wrong to be offended? Well, yes – anybody who complains about me, obviously. But, joking aside, we have had some ridiculous complaints, and, trust me, the BBC take them all very seriously. This sometimes gets right on my tits, as it's often just somebody who is too sensitive. But does that mean that they're wrong? Well, no, it doesn't. But does it also mean that what I said was offensive, because one person believed that they indeed were offended? As I said, it's an ongoing battle.

Another problem we have is dealing with the wonderful world of the media, the tabloid newspapers being the main enemy. They argue that they are reporting on the news and issues of the day. Fair enough, but it's the way they do it that is sometimes infuriating. Sometimes they will add their opinion to the story; other times they won't.

Halle Berry came on the show with Hugh Jackman to promote the new *X-Men 3* movie. Halle was late but Hugh was on time, so we were able to prepare him for the show, but we were left with little time to prep Halle. We prep EVERY guest who comes on the show, even if they listen every day, but all the more so if they are not familiar with our style.

Hugh dived straight in and was asking me about *X Factor* and really getting involved in the show. Halle was pretty much just sitting there and chipping in with 'oh yeah' or 'wow' comments. So I felt it'd be better to focus on him. We got talking about whether or not I could act, and the fact that my voice had appeared in a couple of films. I said that if they were ever looking for a slightly chubby English guy for one of their movies, I was available.

I then moved my attention to Halle to try and get some conversation out of her. I ran through some of the work she had done in the past, and I told her I loved a lot of the movies she had been in. We joked about the Bond movie *Die Another Day*, and I told Hugh he could be a great Bond and he said I could be his Bond double.

I then put on an American voice and said:

'Put your hands up in the air.'

'You're a Brooklyn Bond?' asked Hugh as Halle laughed.

'I'm a black American guy. Big fat black guy. "Put your hands in the air, I don't wanna be shooting your ass."'

They both laughed and Halle asked, 'Are we having a racist moment here?'

'No, not at all. I can't do American voices.' Halle laughed and I continued: 'I could play an English guy,' and then I put on a posh English accent and said, '"Put your hands in the air." But I don't know.'

'Well, you've got to work up to it,' said Hugh. 'Let Daniel do it first and then let him do a couple and then take over.'

We then chatted about whether Daniel Craig would be a good Bond and what the film was all about. Hugh said that he'd heard I don't want to visit Australia. I asked Halle if she'd been there and she told me she was beaten up by a cab driver in Australia.

'For no real reason, just got punched in the face. I mean, when I say I got beat up, I got beat up by a cab driver in Australia.'

We joked about tipping cab drivers and she told me that she didn't get cabs in Australia any more, not that I can blame her. We chatted about where they were going next to promote the movie and if they had to sit through every single premiere and watch the movie again and again. I said come back any time and best of luck with the movie. Then they both left.

Off the air everybody in the studio was bothered by the 'racist' comment. Nobody thought I had said anything racist and the text messages from our audience were all asking what had happened. After the next record we discussed the racist question from Halle and the fact that she didn't get as involved as Hugh did in the conversation. I told everybody to go and see the movie anyway and how I was even going to see it myself. (One of the reasons I was nice about the film was because I'd heard Radio 1 was going to have an exclusive preview of it later in the week. Later that day, the exclusive screening was cancelled. Whoops – that'll be my fault then!) I was moaning about Halle because I knew what would happen the next day in the paper. Knowing how they work, I predicted that the headline would include the words MOYLES and RACIST, and I was right.

MOYLES 'RACIST' SLUR

said the headline in the *Sun*.

Now to everybody who didn't hear the interview it looks like I've made racist comments. She didn't walk out or throw her hands in the air, but that doesn't matter, now some people will refer to me as a racist. I would hate to think I had made a comment that could be deemed as racist, because I'm not racist. However, now the words have been printed in the paper, some people will think I am. When you try to explain about things like this, I always think it sounds like you're excusing yourself, but I honestly don't think about the colour of people's skin. This may sound a bit hippy-like, but if you're nice, then you're nice. If you're horrible, then you're horrible. Male or female, gay or straight, black or white, I don't care. I take people on what they're like. And of course if they listen to the show, then I love them!

Next I was accused of being homophobic.

It was my brother's birthday and we were having a lunch with him and a group of his friends. One of them says:

'That "gay" thing in the paper is silly.'

I had no idea what she was talking about.

'What gay thing?' I asked.

She pulled a copy of the *Metro* paper out of her bag and showed me a story with the headline: '**MOYLES – THAT RINGTONE'S GAY**'.

> *BBC bosses have ruled the word 'gay' now means 'rubbish' in the schoolyard and is fine to use on air. The corporation made the decision after a caller complained, following DJ Chris Moyles's comment that a ringtone was 'gay'.*
>
> *A BBC panel, which includes former Royal Ballet dancer Deborah Bull, ruled, 'The word "gay" is often now used to mean lame or rubbish. This is the widespread current usage of the word amongst young people.'*
>
> *The controversial Moyles did not get off scot-free, though, with the panel instructing him to choose his words more carefully in future.*

I didn't actively recall saying it, and I hadn't been informed that a complaint had been discussed by a BBC panel, let alone that a decision had then been made and an instruction issued for me to choose my words carefully. I shrugged it off and ordered my food.

Over the next few months, this story just wouldn't go away. It even resulted in people marching at Gay Pride holding banners saying '**SACK CHRIS MOYLES**'. I was never questioned about it, or asked to explain or defend myself, yet people were writing articles in various newspapers about the whole issue: just because of this one throwaway (and forgotten by me) comment. Some journalists were saying how I shouldn't be employed and that I was causing hurt and distress to young gay people. Then one person wrote about how outrageous it was that the BBC was allowed to promote and broadcast homophobia on the licence-fee-payers' airwaves.

HOLD ON A SECOND.

I'm not homophobic and I certainly do not promote homophobia. If you've got a problem with me using the word 'gay' to describe something as being a bit pants, then fair enough, but don't accuse me of hating gay people.

But this is the point. A lot of people have no intention of asking me what I really feel about the issue …

BECAUSE THEY DON'T CARE WHAT I THINK.

They use me to get publicity for their organisations. Or they use me as a headline in their paper. They don't seem to want to help matters; merely to point the finger. They will continue to use my name, but have no interest in knowing what I think.

Ben Summerskill is the chief executive of Stonewall, the gay rights campaign organisation. I don't recall having ever met him, and he has never approached me, yet this man has promoted Stonewall on the back of my name. He has written several articles in which he has accused me of being homophobic. If he wanted to know what I think, why hasn't he asked me?

A lot of stuff written about me is either untrue or taken out of context. Now, people who dislike me will say that I'm moaning, but I have a right to reply. So I go on the air and say that I'm getting annoyed at all the reports in the paper about me being homophobic. I explain that one person in particular has been using me to gain publicity and not once have they actually asked me about it directly.

'What do these people want me to say?' I yelled on air. 'Do they want me to say, "Yes, I am homophobic. I don't like the gays." It's ridiculous. Sorry but it just does my head in.'

I then joked about Aled, saying that we even had a token gay working on the show.

To my absolute amazement, Ben Summerskill took what I had said sarcastically, took what I was trying to hold up to ridicule for the absurd notion it was, and used it as a quote to back up his accusations. This is what he wrote in the *Guardian*.

> *Twelve months after 24-year-old Jody Dobrowski was kicked to death on Clapham Common in London just for being gay, the Radio 1 DJ Chris Moyles is still broadcasting to 6 million young people, undermining the confidence of those growing up gay themselves and exculpating those growing up to be homophobic. 'Yeah, I'm homophobic, I don't like the gays,' he snorts proudly. 'Sorry, it just does my head in. We have a token gay on the show!'*

You're linking what I said about a ringtone to the brutal murder of somebody?

ARE YOU OUT OF YOUR FUCKING MIND?

Does this seemingly intelligent man really associate me with somehow condoning some cowardly murderer?

WHO THE FUCK DO YOU THINK YOU ARE?

Perhaps typing away on a keyboard about a DJ who described a ringtone as 'gay' isn't the best way to tackle the issue of brutal gay murders?

And by the way, I don't fucking *snort*, thank you very much.

A spokesperson for Stonewall than gave a quote about me, saying:

> Chris Moyles is not helping young LGBT people struggling to come out through his comments.

Am I meant to be the man who helps lesbian, gay, bisexual and transgender people come out of the closet? No, I'm not. I'm a DJ in the morning on the radio, for Christ's sake, and I don't care if you're gay or straight or whatever you are. I don't care. Are some people offended by my humour about the subject? It would seem that way, yes, and I'm sorry if anybody takes offence, but let's all calm down for one second, please. I am not homophobic. Besides, doesn't that word mean that I have a fear of gay people?

OH MY GOD, THE GAY PEOPLE ARE COMING. RUN FOR YOUR LIVES.

Give me a break.

Then I read this quote from Mr Summerskill:

> *Moyles himself likes to suggest that he is some sort of embattled martyr. (Although no one thinks that he should be locked up – except possibly in a gym.)*

Oh, I see. So it's not OK to refer to something that's rubbish as being gay, as that might offend gay people, but it's absolutely fine to make jokes about my weight. Does Mr Summerskill not care about how many young children at school are bullied because of their weight? Well, of course he was only joking, just making a little joke. He didn't mean to offend anybody. A joke is a joke, isn't it?

Incidentally, Aled and I have spoken a lot about this subject and he feels comfortable working with me because he knows I'm not homophobic. As a man who is proud to be gay, he's annoyed by these accusations himself because he feels they reflect on him. If I'm homophobic, then that implies he works with somebody who doesn't respect him – and what would that say about his own self-respect?

Like everybody on our show, Aled has no problem with parts of his personality being used to get a gag out of: be it his hairy legs, the fact that he is Welsh, or indeed his sexuality. He is comfortable because he knows that I respect him both professionally and, more importantly, personally. Aled is a friend of mine who is gay and I am happy to take the piss out of him, in the same way that he can take the piss out of me.

But as I say, all of this doesn't matter, because it only gets in the way of using my name to write whatever they want.

Meanwhile, I have come out of the closet and am living with a young man called Brian. We rent a weekend cottage in the country-side. It's good to move on.

So when is funny not funny? Answer, when it isn't.

Not very clear, is it? Basically my rule of thumb is that jokes are funny until they're aimed at you.

FEARNE COTTON ON MOYLES

Whenever I see Chris I'm always greeted with this huge great hug, which is so lovely until he ruins it by pretending to stick his tongue down my throat! This is the sort of relationship Christopher and I have. He pretends he wants to snog me and I don't pretend to tell him to bog off! He is one big flirt, that's for sure.

One of my fave Mr Moyles' memories is when our families battled it out on *Family Fortunes*. In rehearsals the Cottons were all quite appalling but come show-time we were on fire! We won by quite a stretch and although Chris would love to say they lost all in the name of comedy, he knows deep down the Cottons rock!!! He did totally win over my family, though, who adore him in every way. This is how it works with everyone. No matter how mouthy you may think Chris is on the radio, when you meet him, he's the kindest, softest sweetie-pie on earth. (Who is still quite gobby and a bit of a perv!)

15

MY SUPERHERO LIFE OF FAME, XBOX AND MATES

I have always been grateful for a lot of different things. I'm grateful my local pub sells Carling lager. It doesn't taste strong and when I drink a few pints I don't feel too bad the next day. I'm grateful that I live near work so occasionally when I'm maybe a bit tired and I don't get out of bed till 6.30 I'm still on time for the start of the show. (Incidentally, this seems to happen after drinking more than a few pints of Carling in my local pub!) I am also very grateful for the amazing double life I lead. It's hardly a superhero's life, but it is still, to me anyway, fascinating in its opposites.

Let me explain. Because of my job on the radio I have met many famous and talented people. Some of these I get to know quite well, some even become friends. I also get a lot of perks such as free this and free that. My fingers are now tapping away on my free MacBook Pro (Thanks, Apple!). Free stuff gets sent to famous people all the time. I've realised that the more famous and rich a person is, the less money they actually have to spend because they get sent so much free stuff. If you're slightly famous but not that rich, you might get the odd freebie. Maybe a two-for-one pass at Alton Towers. If you're VERY famous and EXTREMELY rich, they'll open Alton Towers exclusively for you! (I must point out I have just made that up as an example. If you are actually famous and rich, please don't call up Alton Towers and ask them to open up exclusively for you. They might tell you to piss off!)

Anyway, I get a bit of free stuff from time to time and I know some famous people. I also live a fairly quiet life with a few select friends who occasionally come out to dinner with us or pop round for a brew. I go to my local pubs and eat in my local restaurants. Occasionally I venture into 'town', as I call it; I believe the London locals call it the 'West End', but that really is quite occasionally. My life isn't that Rock and Roll. Here is what I do most days.

I finish the show and maybe have a meeting with the team, then head home about lunchtime. I come home most days and straight away put the kettle on, sit on the couch and play Xbox. Then I feel a bit guilty so I wash up. Bored of that I sit back down on the couch and watch something on TV that I Sky-plussed the night before. Get up, dry the dishes, get bored of that then maybe make a few phone calls. As I'm chatting I start to put the dishes away, finish the call and then straight back to the couch to put the Xbox back on. I am indeed boring. My life often mirrors that of a student with one lecture a week. I run out of fags, so I stick my coat on and head out to the shop.

Then, just like a superhero, my life will change and I am chatting with Chris Martin about a new restaurant down the road as Gwyneth Paltrow is backing the car out of the drive. I walk to the shop and bump into Billie Piper, who hasn't seen me for a while, then eventually start making my way home when Rachel texts me to remind me that Russell Brand, Heidi from the Sugababes and Kimberley from Girls Aloud are all on the show tomorrow with Kelly Osbourne on the day after. I read the text, delete it and then stick the Xbox back on.

My life swings back and forth from normality to showbiz luvvie as fast as David Walliams swings from moody to outrageous camp!

But I LOVE it this way and wouldn't have it any different. It keeps me grounded and it keeps me who I am. Surround yourself with what I call normal down-to-earth people and it keeps you normal. (I once joked on the air about calling them 'normos' and Dave has never let me forget it!) Surround yourself with showbiz people and you lose your grip on reality and become a dick who doesn't know what a pint of milk costs. Obviously I don't, my milk is delivered by helicopter. The balance is just about right for me and I remain pretty much the same boy who arrived in London in 1996.

I'm very conscious about staying down-to-earth. Sometimes you hear about somebody who has achieved a certain amount of fame, or, as is often the case, not achieved it but got it anyway. Most people are pleased for them and feel a bit proud. Then they hear that this particular person has gone and got their big fat head firmly shoved right up their own arse. Straight away the pride turns to disappointment and the inevitable words 'They've changed' are used.

I don't want this to happen to me. If I'm careful, it won't, but the truth is that it's easy to change and become an arse. Trust me, I've seen it enough times. Being on the radio and interviewing bands for enough years, you see pop stars come and go. The first time you meet them they may be shy. The second time you meet them, their confidence is growing and they understand the business a bit more. Then they turn up for an interview late, don't apologise and spend the rest of it moaning about how tired they are and how nobody understands the pressure they're under with a new album to promote. Now this may be true. They might be under a hell of a lot of pressure, but nobody likes a moaner. Besides, they're still like you and me. They still shit the same and have to wipe their arse!

But you get used to the life you have, and if your life is success and praise, eventually you get used to that. It's easy to believe your own hype and change because of it.

In other words, it's easy to become an arsehole!

I'm lucky because as much fun as it is meeting famous people at some cool showbiz party, I have NOTHING to say to these people. Seriously, I am virtually socially inadequate. I can talk to my friend Jodie about anything. I can meet my neighbour Tim for a pint and talk about all sorts of things, but what the fuck do I have in common with Bono?

'I'm flying in our private jet to LA tomorrow to start our world tour.'

'Oh right, nice one. I'm playing my mate Martin on Call of Duty on Xbox Live!'

No, these things aren't for me. I always feel awkward at parties and events like that anyway, so what I choose to do is not bother going. Simple.

Not that I don't have friends who are well known or, dare I say it, 'famous'.

One day my friend Sandy was meeting me at my flat so we could drive to Leeds together. This is the Sandy I make my jingles with. (Yeah, he does most of the work, but hey it's still a team effort.) Anyway it turned out that day that my friend Jodie was working with Fran Healy from Travis and they were both just down the road from where I lived so they decided to pop round for a cup of tea. Fran had never been to my place before and we hadn't seen each other for quite a while. (Incidentally, Fran and I had met a few times before but it was with my mother, once again, that he bonded. I still feel to this day that to Fran I am just a poor second best to my mother.) So Sandy knocks on the door and I bring him into the flat. He sees Sophie and says hello and then turns to see Fran sitting on the couch next to Jodie.

'Oh hello,' says Sandy with a shocked look on his face.

'Sandy, you know Jodie don't you? And this is Fran.'

'Yeah, I know who you are. You're on the cover of one of my favourite albums!'

Sandy and I constantly take the piss out of each other about meeting famous people. I always try to be cool because they're normal people too. Sandy, however, will often get overexcited and say uncool things like:

> 'Oh wow, David Walliams. I saw you buy a newspaper once in my local shop!'
>
> 'Oh really?'

Not the best conversation opener, but it worked out fine in the end.

We said our goodbyes and got in the car for our journey to Leeds.

'You're so showbiz, Chris, do you know that?' Sandy said.

'I am not. I'm just me,' I argued. 'I've known Fran for a few years and he was down the road with Jodie so he popped in for a brew.'

'Oh right. And that's not showbiz, is it? I walk into your flat and there's the lead singer of Travis sitting on your couch having a cup of tea?'

'Well I didn't have any coffee!' I replied.

Most of my friends in London are not well known. It is true to say that most of them do, however, work in this silly media world. One of my friends is a producer with *Richard and Judy*. (Yes, I have met them, and no, they haven't sat on my couch!) Another friend works for a record company. My neighbour is a colourist, whatever the hell that is. I think he colours in the sky on holiday shows or something. We all live near each other and we all have things in common, but the reason I'm FRIENDS with them is because they are nice, genuine, down-to-earth, honest, good people and I like them. Sometimes I'll interview somebody famous and we'll get on really well. Occasionally I become pals with them, and every once in a blue moon, mates. I have a tier system of friendship.

FRIENDS

These are my closest circle. The ones who have seen me dribble kebab down my shirt when I'm drunk and the ones I know I could call in the middle of the night if I ever needed their help. They are all different and I love all of them.

MATES

These are people I really like but don't see enough of to call them a proper friend. If I called them in the middle of the night they would either be flattered that I trusted them enough to call, or they would think it was a bit odd, but still fine.

PALS

Again, I like these people, but I don't know where they live. If we ever bump into each other we would say hello and maybe have a couple of pints. If I called them in the middle of the night, they would ask who I was.

SHOWBIZ PALS

We have met a few times. We got on. We never see each other, but if we do we would say hello. I would NEVER call these people in the middle of the night because I don't have their phone numbers!

And that's another weird thing. I often meet people and we end up swapping numbers. Sometimes it might be somebody from a band I like or a comic who's been on the show and we got on well. Most of the time it's been during a drinking session and numbers get swapped at the peak of the evening while we discuss 'doing this again some time'.

Once again, I'll be honest. Sometimes I forget I have their number and they ask me why I've never called them the next time we meet. I always put that down to drink! Or it may be that they've forgotten we swapped numbers. (Ricky Wilson from the Kaiser Chiefs has given me his number three times now. I put that down to drink too!) Other times I've called them and they have never answered. The worst is when I have put the name in my phone as a code. I do this in case I ever lose my mobile. I know of somebody who lost their phone which had a list of numbers that included me and Zoë Ball and Andi Peters, all under the names 'Chris Moyles', 'Zoë Ball' and 'Andi Peters'. The phone got nicked, and we all got phone calls at two in the morning from a drunk bloke asking if we were who he thought we were. So I'll put numbers in my phone under an easy-to-remember nickname or initial. The only problem is when it's late and I'm a bit tired. I forget who the hell 'P' is. Do I really have a number for Mickey Mouse? And why does my phone say I've just had a text from 'man in the band'? What man? What bloody band?

My friends are everything to me, whether they are well known or not. It's nice to get dressed up and go to a gig and have a drink with the band after the show, but it's equally nice to get dressed up and head for Sunday lunch with Jodie and Abbie. This is what happens when you have a superhero-style showbiz life. Partly famous by day and just another mate at night.

The nice thing is that I know I'm not the only one. I was once at the bar of my local pub when Jimmy Carr walked in and stood next to me.

'Hello, Chris. What are you doing in here?'

'What am I doing in here? This is my local! What are you doing in here?'

'Well I came to watch the football with my mates but I think I have the wrong pub.'

Two partly famous people in one pub at the same time would be like crossing the streams in the *Ghostbusters* movie. As Egon said, there would be *total protonic reversal* and *all life as you know it would stop instantaneously and every molecule in the body would explode at the speed of light.*

OK, so maybe it wouldn't be as bad as that!

16

MEET THE FAMILY

talk about my family on the radio and I've written about them already, but I'm still constantly being asked about them. I'm not sure whether it's because people think I must be the black sheep of the family, or whether they think all of us have big gobs and big egos. I don't really understand the curiosity about my family life, because my family are pretty much normal. Well, they're as normal as to be expected I suppose.

I am the youngest of two children to very loving parents. My parents are still married, which as you know these days is a feat in itself. I think they only have to stay married for another two years and they win a set of steak knives from the local church.

My mum was christened Hannah Veronica. Everybody calls her Vera for short, but Mum thinks that Vera sounds common, like Vera Duckworth in *Coronation Street*. My mum is a snob, which is where I get it from.

My dad was christened John Christopher. Everybody calls him Chris, which he's fine with. He has no choice really, as most people don't even know that my mum and dad's first names are actually their middle names. My dad is working class, which is where I get those elements from. So basically I am a snobbish working-class northerner with Irish roots. What a combination.

My older brother Kieron has, as far as I'm concerned, a wicked name. It's so different and it stands out. I have met quite a few other Kierons but only one other who spelt it the same as our kid. Christopher is a fine name, don't get me wrong, but there are loads of us, there aren't many of him. Kieron is highly intelligent, which might be why sometimes he is a pain in the arse. I love my brother, I really do. I look up to him, which says a lot, because for the first twelve years of my life he used to enjoy using me as some kind of punchbag. There are many things he has done to me over the years that I have forgiven him for.

THINGS I FORGAVE MY OLDER BROTHER FOR:

PUNCHING ME

I will admit that being the younger brother came with its privileges. Getting away with murder was the best one; ratting on my brother for something far worse than I was about to be told off for was another. However, the rough always comes with the smooth, and for this privilege, came punches. Kieron wasn't a violent boy at all. He wasn't even the typical older brother either, but there were times when he would give me a slap. As we got older, I would occasionally fight back. This was a mistake, because even though I might have been as tough as he was, in my mind I was still the younger brother. If I got a good slap in, or whacked him with a decent punch, the look on his face would scare the crap out of me, and I'd be off like shit off a stick, running up the stairs to lock myself in the bathroom.

DRUGS

Kieron lost his mind one day and decided to be honest with my mum. Oh what a touching moment that must have been. Kieron, for reasons only he knows, chose to tell her he had once tried drugs. Thanks a bundle, older brother. Now I don't do drugs myself. I never have. They just don't interest me. I smoke too much and I drink a lot – that's enough for me. But the fact that Kieron came clean about his Beatles-like experience made it impossible for me even to breathe air without Mum suspecting I was on 'the drugs'.

'Can I ask you a question? Are you on the drugs?' she would ask. 'Now I just want you to be honest with me. It's OK, but are you on the drugs?'

To this day I'm not 100 per cent convinced that Mum doesn't think drugs come in a box with 'The Drugs' written down the side. It became like Mum's personal habit. I'd have a few drinks:

'Are you on the drugs?'

I'd wake up and be tired:

'Are you on the drugs?'

Listen, Mum, I know you're reading this, so please, for the very last time, I am not on the drugs, OK? And no, Viagra doesn't count.

USING ME AS A TOILET

When you're young and you drink too much, it makes you drunk. Sometimes when you're drunk you sleepwalk and don't really know where you are. I feel it necessary to point this out before I continue with the story.

So there I am, asleep in bed one night. Probably dreaming about Debbie Gibson or Pepsi and Shirley or something, when all of a sudden my bedroom door flies open and in walks my brother.

'What are you doing, Kier?' I ask in a half-awake state.

He doesn't answer, and instead continues walking all the way up to the side of my bed, gets Kieron Jnr out and proceeds to take a piss down the side of the bed while I'm lying there. I try to move but the layout of my bedroom only allows me to push against the wall as I try to get away from the spray of my brother's drunken urine. He finishes up, pops the little fella back in his PJ bottoms and leaves my room. I sat in there in silence for about thirty seconds, before: '**MUUUUUUUUUUUUM**!!'

That night I refused to sleep in my own bed. Now, of course, these days I'm only too aware of a situation like this. I call it 'dead man walking' and I'll admit to having done it myself once or twice, although there's never been anybody asleep underneath me! On this occasion I'd only go back to sleep if I could sleep on Mum and Dad's floor, so we put some blankets down and off I went to sleep, wondering why my brother decided to pee on me.

The morning came and breakfast was being served. I had slept like a log since the wee incident, and Mum had left me to have a lie-in. Dad was busy cooking so Mum sent my brother upstairs to wake me up. Not a great idea that one. I woke up to find my brother hovering over me.

'Jesus Christ, not again, what the fuck is wrong with you?' I screamed.

He had no idea, and to this day can't remember it. Dirty boy!

And finally:

TELLING ME WHERE CHRISTMAS PRESENTS CAME FROM

Look, I know I can be cutting occasionally. I know I like to get a laugh from time to time at somebody else's expense. But I also know that I am a big softy. The final thing I forgave my brother for was to do with Christmas presents, and I was so affected by it that I don't want any other child blaming me for finding out what I found out that cold and dark Thursday in December. If you know what I mean, then fine, we'll move on. And if you don't understand what I'm going on about, don't worry about it. Everything is fine, now let's move on anyway, and don't look in that cupboard!

Kieron and I are very different. At school I tried to blend in, while he wore nothing but black for about four years. He would get moody a lot, which looking back was understandable for a man as intelligent as he was having to live with us divvies. He got bored, and strangely enough Mum telling him what was for tea that night and me trying to explain to him the wonders of the TV show *Batfink* were not challenging enough. Let's face it, you'd get bored if you were that clever and had me as a younger brother. He just seemed to know a lot about a lot.

My favourite thing he used to do when we were younger freaked my mum out. We'd be sitting down watching TV and we'd see them at the gate. Often in twos but sometimes, if we were lucky, they'd send just the one. I am referring, of course, to Jehovah Witnesses. Now, I don't care what your thing is. What you believe in, whether you believe or don't believe, is your business, but back then, when I was a kid, these people would knock on the door and try to talk to us about Jesus and how we should be good people. We knew about Jesus. I had an Irish mother, for God's sake. Plus we were good people. I knew this because of the scallies I would hang out with at school. We were a good family, because Dad never came home from work with stolen meat. And Mum didn't fiddle the gas meter. We were good, thanks, and we didn't need lessons.

Knock knock on the front door.

'Hello. I'd like to take some time to talk to you about the good work that Jesus did.'

And that would be about it, before Mum said:

'No, we're fine, thank you. I go to church every Sunday and enjoy my faith. We're just sitting down to our tea. Thank you and good luck.'

And then she would shut the door. She was polite and pleasant in her disinterest. Kieron, on the other hand, liked to talk, and would be only too pleased to get to the door before Mum.

'Hello. I'd like to take some time to talk to you about the good work that Jesus did.'

> 'Actually, I have a few questions about Jesus and the state of religion generally in this country. It seems to me that many people worship the same God, or similar Gods at least. In a world where idols are too easily formed, shouldn't an all-greater being actually *not* be that accessible? To know the truth about life surely is something that mere mortals like ourselves could never easily do.'

And he was off. These poor people, who were only doing their job, would knock on the door and be greeted by a child who not only had questions but had the answers too. They would make their excuses and leave. This kept my brother sane!

In Leeds he went from boring job to boring job before eventually heading down to London. Within weeks he had met a new set of friends, found work and was generally having a better life. London suits my brother. He's always liked it, and now that he has a new girlfriend and a new flat, he isn't going anywhere. His girlfriend has changed him so much it's quite scary, but all for the better. For years Kieron was never interested in learning how to drive.

'Why should I? Everybody I know drives, which means that I can go out, have a few drinks and always get a lift home from somebody.' This was his argument, and it wasn't a bad one. However, now he is a changed man and has even hinted at learning to drive. That's the thing with my brother: he will hold a very strong view on something he could argue about with you for days. Then, if he changes his mind, he still wins, because he just says he's changed his mind. End of argument. I told you he was clever.

I often worry about what Dad must have thought when my brother and me were kids. Here was a tough Leeds man with two sons. Dad loves his football to this day and I am sure he would've been delighted if Kieron or me had gone on to have trials for Leeds United. Sadly for him, neither my brother nor me wanted to play football, we weren't skilled in any way, and we both had ridiculous ideas about getting involved in music. He must have thought we were a right pair of morons. But strangely it was my dad who was cool with the idea of me finishing school and getting a job in radio. Mum naturally wanted me to go to college and get some extra education. She knew that radio was in my blood but she also thought – and I don't blame her – that I needed qualifications in case things didn't work out. Dad, however, fully backed me up, saying if that was what I really wanted to do, then I should do it. A very brave man who had worked his balls off for years to keep a roof over our heads. I'm not so sure I would be as tolerant in his position. But they both have been and continue to be so supportive of my career, and it really helps.

Dad's life was very different to mine, but strangely he and I are very similar. I certainly get my stubbornness from him, but I get my sense of humour from him too. He's a quick-witted man, and I mean quick. He can carry a tune and has recently taken up playing the banjo. If he had tried, I have no doubt he could have become a famous comic. It's not that he's a joke teller. He's not one of those blokes sitting at family parties and making everybody laugh. Dad is secretly funny. He'll chip away over time so that he doesn't have to tell a joke, it could merely be a raised eyebrow or a throwaway comment. Either way, he's a funny man, and once you get to know him, you'll see it.

When he was younger he worked in a foundry. I don't even know what one of them is but it sounds like proper graft. He would work hard, get paid and then spend his money. He and his brother Jim would go out drinking, like normal brothers would. But Dad always seemed to have a new car. When we go out and we pass classic cars, Dad will be like, 'I used to have one of those.' Cars were either a lot cheaper those days or he and Jim were bloody car thieves!

He played football with Jim as well. I have always known this but it wasn't until I started drinking with Dad and his brother that I found out the pair of them were little buggers on the pitch. We'd end up in a pub somewhere in Leeds, and it could be anywhere, but chances are they'd know somebody there.

'Bloody hell, I don't believe it. It's the Moyles brothers,' some old bloke would say. 'I remember these two knocking the shit out of me on the football pitch.'

Dad would give me one of those 'oh don't listen to him' looks. But I was hooked. 'Tell me more. In fact, let me buy you a drink.'

Dad would be embarrassed but Jim loved it.

When my dad met my mum and got married, he calmed down. Not that he was a thug, it was just that now he was a married man. He got a job working for the Post Office and he stayed there until he retired. He loved his job because he loved driving, but he worked long, hard hours. Something I have become allergic to since I started work. The nice thing about Dad driving at night was that occasionally I went with him. For one night only it was really exciting. Go to the main sorting office in Leeds and fill up the lorry with all the mailbags. Drive to Newcastle and swap vans with the man who drove down from Scotland. Take the new mail back to Leeds, empty the van and then go home. Long hours, as I said, but he loved it.

The other nice thing was that Dad knew everywhere. When we went for a drive out to the countryside, Dad would find all these weird and wonderful little villages. He also knew most of the pubs, despite not being a massive drinker. I think this was because the post-boxes or post offices were often next to the pub – or at least I like to think that!

It wasn't just trips to the countryside. The man loves driving so we'd jump in the car at the slightest excuse and head off anywhere. Dad was like early sat nav. He always knew the way, and he knew the exact time we'd arrive.

'If we leave now we'll be there by four o'clock.'

And sure enough, no matter what traffic there was, or if we had to stop for a pee, we'd arrive at exactly four o'clock. No matter how far we were going, there was one rule, and one rule only.

WE DON'T STOP AT THE SERVICES.

And we never did. Ever. Now I stop at the services even if I don't want anything. I do it just because I can. I swear Dad used to see these places as evil.

'What do you wanna stop at the services for?'

'So we can get some food and drink,' we'd plead.

'There's drink in the bag and some sandwiches that your

mother made before we got in the car. And besides, if we stop you'll be playing those bloody machines and we'll be in there for half an hour.'

'But, Dad, I want a KFC.'

'A KFC? A KFC? What do you think I am, made of money? They're a bloody rip-off place, those services. Everything is over-priced, and besides, your mother made those sandwiches and they better be bloody eaten or that's another waste of money. Tuna doesn't grow on trees you know!'

We may have been going where the sun shone brightly, but we weren't going to stop and get a KFC on the way.

I love my dad a lot. I know that if I ever have kids, I'd like to be the kind of dad to them my dad was to me. It's just a shame that he'll never get to see them, as I plan to have children at about the same age Charlie Chaplin had his.

I also love the fact that Mum and Dad are still married and, seemingly, very happy. Personally, if I had to live with either of them, I'd've gone mad by now. The pair of them together are like Bert and Ernie from *Sesame Street*, but it works and you can't deny it.

Now what could I possibly say about my mum that hasn't been said before? She's 'quiet' would be one thing. Because she isn't. She likes to talk does my mum. She talks to her husband, she talks to the TV, she even talks to herself!

Mum was born in Dublin and is from a typical Irish family. There are bloody loads of them, and to make matters worse, there's only one brother. Poor sod! Mum coming from Ireland has had quite an effect on me. First, I love the place. I'm not there enough and would love to spend more time over there. The people are great, the drinking is great, you just can't fault the place. The only thing about Dubliners is their language. It's fruity, to say the least. Now I don't mind because I swear like a trooper, as my mum would say. All my cousins swear, my friends swear, so it's not a problem to me. However, Mum has never liked it. Which is a bit odd, when you come from a place where a typical conversation contains all manner of swear words, including fuck, arse, Jesus and bollocks, or a combination of all of them. This leads to a brilliant problem between my mother and me.

You may have heard the word 'feck' used before. To me, this is an Irish version of the word 'fuck'. However, to my mother, it is most certainly not like that word. Strange, as its usage almost mirrors the traditional 'fuck'. Let me now give you a lesson in:

MY MUM, AND THE 'FECK' WORD.

For example, my mother would say if she cut her finger:

'Oh feck it!'

This, according to my mum's rules, is not swearing.

Another time she might be having a good old bitch about somebody. Let's just say that a suggestion has been made that this person could pop round for tea. Now Mum doesn't agree with this idea. In that case, it could sound like this:

'She can in her fecking mind.'

Again, to Mum, it isn't bad language. So as a child this was very confusing to me, especially when Mum caught me telling somebody to 'FECK OFF!'

'You shouldn't use words like that, Christopher.'

'Words like what? You use them,' I said.

'I certainly do not use words like that,' said Mum, forgetting that I lived in the same house as she did.

'Yes, you do. You said *feck* yesterday when you pricked your finger with the knitting needle.'

'Oh that's different,' said Mum. 'In Ireland, *feck* isn't a swear word.'

'Mum, are you insane, it's just the word *fuck* but pronounced slightly different.'

'Don't you be using language like that in my house.'

'But you use it all the time and you just try and act like it isn't the same word. Which it is, by the way. And also, this is my house too,' said me, like a proper child.

'Oh feck off. May God forgive me!'

Which is another thing too. I would get told off for swearing, yet if Mum ever swore, she just said, 'May God forgive me,' as if that made it all right. Mum was, and still is, very religious, so she must have insider information. As well as this she would say, 'Jesus, Mary and Joseph.' This was Mum's version of 'Oh Fucking Hell!'

I remember being a smart arse once when I was trying to get out of going to church.

'Yeah, well, why should I go?' I argued. 'There are things in the Church that I don't agree with, and that would make me a hypocrite if I went, wouldn't it?' A fair point, which I think I argued quite well. But once again, like with most things in life, I was wrong.

Mum simply looked at me and said, 'You don't have to agree with everything that the Church tells you.'

Mum explained that her religion was very personal to her. She believed in the Church but did not necessarily agree with all its teachings. For example, Mum doesn't have a problem with homosexuality, which the Church does. Or with divorce. 'I take from the Church what I want to take from it. I enjoy my religion and it is special to me, but I still believe in what I believe in.'

How can you fault her? She's got the best of both worlds, and because she's Irish and Catholic, God will probably give her the benefit of the doubt too.

Although God couldn't help Mum with everything.

Up until recently Mum didn't grasp the whole voicemail thing. When I first moved to London I lived in a big flat. It was huge. When the phone rang, by the time I got to it I'd often missed the caller. I explained to Mum one day that it was probably worth her while to wait for the answerphone beep to go off, and then to say, 'Hello, are you in, it's your mum,' in case I am running down the corridor to the phone.

I said, 'Sometimes, if I'm in, I can hear the machine, so just chat for a few seconds and I might pick up. If I don't, then it means I'm out.'

And so she did. Every message I got from her on the machine would be like this:

> 'Hello, Christopher, it's your mum. Hello? Hello, are you there? Can you hear me? Hello? Are you in the flat or are you out? I can't hear anything. I wonder if he can hear me. Hello? Hello? No, he can't hear me, he must be out.'

And the phone would go dead.

Sometimes, however, I'd be in and it would work like a charm. However, Mum had no idea that mobile-phone voicemails worked in a different way. After a meeting one afternoon I switched my mobile on, only to get this message from Mum:

> 'Hello, Christopher, it's your mum. Hello? Hello, are you there? Can you hear me? Hello? Are you out? I can't hear anything, I wonder if he can hear me. Hello? Hello? No, he can't hear me, he must be out. But I'm ringing his mobile so why doesn't he have it with him?'

Mum also has a problem with writing down phone numbers. It's something I am sure will eventually come to us all, but at the moment I am fine at hearing a phone number and then writing it down. Now I don't think this is an age thing. Writing-down-phone-number-itis knows no age, race or creed. It can strike you while you are young or wait until you get older. The man who answers the phone at my local curry house has got it, and now, sadly, Mum has it. She has to repeat every single digit to you very slowly, no matter how short the number.

'OK, you got a pen, Mum? Good, it's oh-seven-eight-seven-one.'

'Hang on a second. Oh. Seven. Eight. Seven. What was it?'

'One, Mum. One.'

'OK, that's oh. Seven. Eight. Seven. Double one.'

'No, not double one, just one.'

This has been known to go on for days.

Most regular listeners will know about my mum's love of festivals and hanging out backstage. She's been to so many gigs and hung out with so many bands that she's almost part of the event. At the Leeds festival, everybody knows who she is, and those who don't, want to get to know her.

'Is that your mum?' I get asked.

'Yeah it is,' I say proudly.

'She is wicked. Can I have a photo with her?'

Honestly, Mum gets asked all the time to pose for photos. She should be the famous one, not me. I always say the same thing: 'Well, if she's OK with it, but you'll have to ask her.'

I'm now used to taking second place to my mum. In the early days when she started coming to gigs, I used to get embarrassed. But these days, everybody expects to see her. It used to be a case of me bringing Mum to a gig. Now, Mum asks me if I want tickets. She'll have her access-all-areas pass and will know everybody from the promoter to the security guards.

Melvin Benn is THE man when it comes to festivals. He is the big cheese, the head honcho and the most important at the Reading and Leeds festival. I was staying in the same hotel as him one year and we were chatting at the bar.

'Your mum and dad not here tonight, are they?' he asked.

'No, they're at their house. I'm only staying in the hotel so I could fall into the lift when I've finished in the bar and get taken straight up to my room.'

'Are they coming to the festival tomorrow?' he asked, clearly not interested in me.

'Yeah, they are. Mum really wants to see the Kaiser Chiefs.'

'Well, listen,' said Melvin. 'I've got to visit the site at Reading tomorrow. Do you think your mum and dad would fancy jumping in the helicopter and flying down there with me? Have a look around and a little drink and then we'll fly back to Leeds in time to see the Kaiser Chiefs.'

Bloody hell. What a cool thing to do. Flying between sites at Reading and Leeds, with the bloody organiser, in a bloody helicopter. Bloody hell. I told Mum the next morning.

'Oh that sounds nice, but I think we'll just go up in the car. We've got a VIP car park pass.'

★

I know most sons love their families, and I am no exception. My family has given me unconditional love, help and support throughout my life. I hope I make them proud and that they know how much I love them. I know there have been times in the past, and I'm sure there will be in the future, when they've worried about choices I've made, but they ALWAYS support me. I have NEVER been embarrassed at showing my feelings towards my family. My brother and I have always hugged the living daylights out of each other, and Mum has told me EVERY DAY OF MY LIFE that she loves me. I kiss my dad every time I see him, which isn't always easy when there's a lot of stubble going on. I feel blessed to have such a loving and friendly family and I love them all so much. However, if they think they're getting any more bloody money out of me, then they can all FECK OFF!

FRAN HEALY ON MOYLES

When I first heard Chris on the radio, I was shocked at all the dead air he would inject into his show. These long pregnant silences on prime-time radio made my shoulders tense and were at odds with all the other shows running at the time. He was so gobby and cheeky, I was convinced he was gonna be difficult if I ever met him. So when I did finally meet Chris I was shocked ... here was this lippy disc jockey and he's all 'Hey, come and meet ma mum ... she's over here and is dying to meet you ...' In the short walk from our stage to the foyer of the venue my whole perception of him was shattered. He was the sweetest man I think I have met in all my years in the music business. Plus his mum and the rest of the family were the loveliest folks. Vera, his mum, reminded me of Martin Scorsese's mum who does cameos in his movies like *Goodfellas*. You look at the backstage areas of big outdoor shows, full of bands and liggers all hanging out, posing, and then there's this wee Irish lady standing in the mayhem, chewing the fat with some guy with red spiky hair like she was talking to her next-door neighbour, as normal as you like. In the years that have followed, I have seen her at every Radio 1 gig, chatting to the stars, making everyone feel at home backstage. They say the fruit doesn't fall far from the tree. When you meet Vera it's easy to see why Chris has connected so well with people.

17

THERE IS NO CARRY ON IN EASTENDERS

For those of you who don't know, *EastEnders* is a popular soap opera on BBC television here in The UK. (I'm explaining this for any readers from America or Canada, and on the off-chance my book ends up in a *Blue Peter* Time Capsule.) The rest of you know the idea. It's the everyday tale of miserable cockneys and their extraordinary 'normal' lives. In any six weeks in that strange little square you can expect at least one of the following:

A robbery storyline

A murder storyline

A 'gay' storyline

A step-brotherly-love storyline

A slight racism storyline

A young-girl-gets-pregnant-and-loses-the-baby, or gives-it-up-for-adoption or keeps-it-and-upsets-her-family storyline

Yet these bizarre Londoners STILL insist on living there. Morons.

There are many other strange things. For example, Frank's used-car lot. It's sat in the corner for years, yet nobody EVER buys a car. Add to that the fact that Phil Mitchell owns a car-fixing garage and has ALWAYS got work. How? Whose cars is he fixing?

My favourite one was when Steve Owen moved into the square. Here was a man we were meant to believe was a clever, street-wise businessman making a good bit of money and wearing nice suits. Yet he chose to live in an East End shit hole. Yeah, right. No offence to anybody living in a place similar to Albert Square, but let's be honest, if you can afford a wardrobe of expensive suits, you can afford to live somewhere better than next door to Pat Butcher!

The other thing about Steve Owen was the fact that he was played by an actor. I know we're meant to suspend disbelief when watching a soap opera. Remember, this is 'Real Life' we're talking about. But I could NEVER get over the fact that Steve Owen ... used to be in Spandau Ballet! Or did he? In *EastEnders* he wasn't Martin Kemp, he was 'Steve Owen' who turned the Market Cellar into e20. And this opens up a huge 'Fact Vortex' ...

One Christmas I was sat in my front room in Leeds with the rest of my family watching the Christmas Day edition of *EastEnders*. Their day was very similar to mine. Woke up, opened some presents. Just like Ian Beale and his kids. Left Mum cooking the Christmas dinner as me, Dad and Kieron had a few pints in our local. Just like the people in *EastEnders*. Then it's back home for dinner before collapsing on the couch to watch *EastEnders*. Just like ... oh no, hang on. They can't watch *EastEnders* in *EastEnders*. That couldn't work. And because they don't want you to turn over yet, the characters can't even rush home to watch *Coronation Street*. This is when the 'Fact Vortex' comes into effect. Actual 'Real Life' doesn't exist in the

TV world of *EastEnders*, it can't do. So with this in mind, if Steve Owen is played by Martin Kemp from Spandau Ballet, then Spandau Ballet NEVER existed.

Now strap yourselves in because this gets VERY confusing.

Peggy Mitchell is NOT Barbara Windsor, so you can forget the *Carry On* films. Mark Fowler couldn't have been Todd Carty, who was brilliant as Tucker in *Grange Hill*. And as his sister Michelle Fowler was played by Susan Tully who was also from *Grange Hill*, then that definitely rules out that show. So no *Carry On* movies, no Spandau Ballet and no *Grange Hill*.

BUT IT GETS WORSE.

Tamzin Outhwaite played Melanie Owen. She went on to appear in ITV's *Red Cap* and later BBC1's *Hotel Babylon*, so they now don't exist in *EastEnders* either. Her father in the show was played by Leslie Schofield, who was in a ton of great television shows and movies. He famously played the dad in the kids' TV show *Jonny Briggs*, but even worse, he was in the original *Star Wars* movie, playing Chief Bast in the Death Star.

So to recap, in the 'real life' world of *EastEnders*, there is no:

Spandau Ballet

Carry On movies

Grange Hill

Star Wars

Now let's throw in John Bardon, who plays Dot's fella Jim Branning. He's been in *Lovejoy*, *Only Fools and Horses* and *Dad's Army*.

Perry Fenwick plays Billy Mitchell. Perry is a fine actor who has starred in *Bergerac*, *Inspector Morse* and *Minder*.

In *EastEnders*, Derek Martin is Charlie Slater. Derek was previously in *The Sweeney* and the rubbish BBC1 Spanish soap *Eldorado*. (So there's some good news at least!)

Pauline Fowler was played by Wendy Richard from *Are You Being Served?* And she was also in some *Carry On* movies, but then again Barbara Windsor has cancelled them out so it doesn't matter.

For music fans, Phil Daniels plays Kevin Wicks. So he could've never appeared on Blur's famous *Parklife*. He was also in some movie called *Quadrophenia*.

So now the list stands at:

Spandau Ballet

Carry On movies

Grange Hill

Star Wars

Lovejoy

Only Fools and Horses

Dad's Army

Bergerac

Inspector Morse

Minder

The Sweeney

Eldorado

Are You Being Served?

And *Quadrophenia!*

Even the dog Wellard appeared in *A Touch of Frost!*

So there you have it. The real world of *EastEnders* that has cancelled out some of my favourite TV shows and movies. All I hope now is they give Johnny Vaughan a job so we can forget about how horrible his TV sitcom was!

18

HELLO, WEMBLEY

Since I began this weird and wonderful career in radio, many fantastic opportunities have come my way. I have also had some shite offered to me as well. Like when I was asked if I wanted to pose naked for the cover of a magazine. At the time I trusted the people around me, who all agreed it would be funny. And they were right, it was indeed funny, but then again they weren't the ones who had to get their face made up to look like a girl and then take their clothes off in front of a photographer with only two strategically placed fans to cover their modesty. Add to that the fact that I am not the thinnest of beings, and it really did make for a gross photo. I remember being stood in the changing room about to walk into the studio where there would be several people waiting for me. I was naked as the day I was born, well, almost, as I had piled on a few stone since. All my clothes that up until one minute earlier had been on my body, now lay over a chair, and as I looked at myself in the mirror, I decided there and then that I did not look good naked.

I also realised that having a huge belly didn't do wonders for my penis size. I'll be honest, I'm hardly hung like a snake down there, and with the impending doom of having to pose naked in front of the camera, poor 'little Chris' had pretty much decided to hibernate. The thought actually crossed my mind that just in case somebody did catch a glimpse, perhaps I should try and at least make the little fella appear to be – how should I put this – slightly more impressive. However, I also didn't want to be seen as being aroused by the imminent naked shoot. I didn't want anybody in the studio thinking that maybe this was all a weird turn-on for me, because:

TRUST ME, IT WASN'T.

Besides, I had a full face of make-up and a massive belly hanging down so nobody was going to see anything anyway. I myself haven't seen my penis without the use of a mirror since 1995!

So naked photo shoots for me are mainly bad. However, live radio shows are mainly good.

I've been lucky enough to be asked to present the radio show live from various different locations, and I'll be honest, flying to Los Angeles, Las Vegas and New York to work is brilliant.

To be in an exciting city broadcasting back to the UK is a challenge. You've got to make sure everybody listening knows you're having a good time, without pissing them off with the fact that while I may be in a beautiful air-conditioned studio with 90-degree sunshine beaming down outside, some of our listeners are stood at work in Tesco in Middlesbrough with the rain pissing down outside.

To be broadcasting by a pool in Portugal or a football stadium in Germany is very cool, and I genuinely always appreciate it. Especially after we have broadcast from not so glamorous locations.

As part of a feature for Radio 1, we were asked to present our show from somewhere different. A place where our audience might spend some of their summer holiday.

'Blackpool,' I said, thinking of donkeys and candyfloss.

'That's already taken, that one.'

'Brighton,' I said, thinking of the end of the pier or a cool bar down by the beach.

'No, we've done that before.'

'Well, where exactly do you have in mind for this exciting broadcast?'

'Butlins in Skegness.'

I thought of firing this person immediately.

After a heavy discussion, we all agreed it would be a good laugh. After the broadcast, we all agreed we were wrong and we should've gone to Brighton. Not that there is anything wrong with Butlins. It's a lovely idea. Families staying in a chalet, or apartments as we were told they're now called. There are bars, and rides for the kids. There's even a bookies, which is brilliant. I mean how many times have you been on your holidays and thought to yourself: 'The sun and the beach are great, but it's just a shame there isn't anywhere I can bet on the 3.30 at Chelmsford'?

But you know, maybe it just wasn't for us. Maybe the fight the night before in the bar put us off slightly, or the fact that we seemed to be the only 'holidaymakers' there without tattoos, and I'm including the kids. We came to the conclusion that it wasn't our 'cup of tea' when the Butlins mascot Billy the Bear came dancing on to the stage, as Dave and myself stood there wearing our redcoats praying for ten o'clock to arrive.

So, yeah, I've been asked to do some odd things, but I have been lucky enough to be asked to do some cool things as well.

I'm sitting at home one day when my agent emails me with a request. In the email she says that I've been asked to do something but it's during a time that I am meant to be on holiday and maybe I won't want to do it. I open the email and read it. I then hit reply and typed

ARE YOU FUCKING KIDDING ME?

I was being asked if I would like to co-host the stage at the new Wembley stadium for the forthcoming Live Earth concert to combat the climate crisis. The brainchild of former American Vice-President Al Gore, this was due to be a massive concert with a line-up that already included Foo Fighters, Metallica and Madonna. There would be three hosts, including comedian and presenter Russell Brand, brilliant American comic Chris Rock, and me. I think Russell is brilliant, and I love Chris Rock, plus I've always joked for years about shouting 'Hello, Wembley!' and now I would get to do it for real.

BUT I was worried that maybe it wasn't true. I mean, if they can get Chris Rock to come over to London to host the show, why would they want me? Sure I can get a crowd going, but did they really want Chris Moyles? I checked and it turned out that they did. This is something I do all the time. As you'll know if you listen regularly to the show, on the air I'm very confident. But in real life, I'm a bit rubbish. My ego is nowhere near as big as it is on the air, so I naturally assume that they have sent the email to the wrong person. But no, they hadn't, and to make things even better, they were excited at the prospect of me doing it.

Initially I was due to host the middle part of the day, from about 4pm till 7pm. However, after a meeting with the organisers, it was decided that I should open the show at 1.30pm, with Genesis the first band on stage. They reckoned 70,000 people would be at the gig, with an audience of millions watching around the world. This was something I couldn't miss, so my holiday got moved and I said YES!

It's always exciting being at any big music event, but to be at the legendary Wembley stadium, home to Live Aid, was going to be amazing. I'd never done anything on this scale before, and since I was writing this book, I took my camera and documented my whole day.

This is what happens when you co-host a huge music concert at a gigantic stadium.

★

Friday 6 July 2007

11.00am

After the radio show I was to be picked up and taken down to Wembley to be shown around and possibly get to sound-check onstage. I leave the Radio 1 building to be met by a guy in a nice Mercedes car which has:

LIVE EARTH – VIP TRANSFER

written down the side. Underneath it says:

POWERED BY SUN DIESEL

I had no idea what that meant but I knew it must be environmentally friendly, as that was what the show was all about.

'What does sun diesel mean, mate?' I asked the driver.

'No idea. I only got the car yesterday. But it seems to drive the same.'

Maybe saving the earth was going to take a little bit more than this.

We arrived at the stadium where cars were already queuing up and security guards were all over the place. A nice Australian girl called Michelle was there to meet me and she gave me my pass to make sure I could actually get in the building. First, though, I had to have a cigarette. The new no-smoking law had just come into effect, and despite Wembley not having a bloody roof, they have banned smoking from the whole place. Still, it was a sunny day and that meant I could soak up the atmosphere a little.

'Now we didn't get a list for your rider. Did you not want anything?' asked Michelle.

For those of you who don't know, a rider is a list of requirements from an artist. Let's say the Rolling Stones are playing and in their dressing rooms they want four bottles of Jack Daniels, one crate of beer and a hundred blue Smarties – that would be their rider. I hadn't given them a list because I only really needed water. I mean, I suppose I could've asked for a tray of Yorkshire puddings and some Toffo, but what would be the point?

'It's just that your dressing room is looking very empty,' said Michelle.

'I have a dressing room?'

I was amazed. I knew I was hosting the first few hours of the show but surely they had bigger fish to fry than me. Shouldn't they be concentrating on Madonna or Duran Duran? Besides, I wouldn't use it much as I'd be stood at the side of the stage for most of the day. We walked down into the underbelly of Wembley stadium. Me and the radio-show team had been invited on a tour of the stadium just before it was finished so I'd already seen how big the place was. Underneath is a long road that runs all the way round. A couple of twists and turns and we were at the side of the stage at the edge of the pitch. Then it was a left and a right, and through some doors to the dressing rooms. And there it was, the very first dressing room on the left, with a sign outside saying who would be in there. Michelle opened the door and then said she'd be back in one minute. The moment she left, I whipped my camera out and took a picture of the room, and, more excitingly for me, the sign on the wall outside. It said:

CELEBRITY HOSTS

And then underneath in alphabetical order:

RUSSELL BRAND

CHRIS MOYLES

CHRIS ROCK

WOW. What a sandwich that was. A dollop of Moyles with some Brand and Rock bread. (Sorry, I'm getting carried away.) I was really excited. Not that they were there or anything. This was the day before and all you could see were security men and workers in luminous work jackets. The whole of Wembley looked like a massive bin-man convention.

'So are any of the bands sound-checking today?' I asked Michelle, knowing full well there would be. When Live 8 was on in Hyde Park, Radio 1 was backstage all day, so the afternoon before we popped down to make sure we knew where to go and all that. Luckily for us, all the sound checks were taking place at the time we were there. It's so cool because it's like a gig in a massive park but with only a few people watching. In a few hours we saw Paul McCartney, Sting and Madonna. My friend Mitch and I were watching McCartney play and when he finished his song, we just started clapping. As we were the only people watching, he looked over at us and pointed, saying:

'Thanks very much, guys.'

By the time Madonna was on, a small crowd had gathered so it actually was a gig, but with lots of stopping and starting.

'Snow Patrol are sound-checking soon and then Spinal Tap I think,' said Michelle.

Now, I LOVE Spinal Tap, the fake band from the *This is Spinal Tap* 'rocumentary' spoof of 1984. A couple of days before they had been at Radio 1 to record an interview with Colin Murray, and as I was such a fan, I waited outside the building so I could get my photo taken with them. Sad, but for me, very cool.

'Shit, I love Spinal Tap. Are they here?' I said, like a girl at a Westlife concert.

'Not sure yet. We can go to their dressing room and have a look if you like.'

I gave the dressing-room trip a miss (I mean, I could hardly knock on the door and say hello, bearing in mind I'd been hanging outside the radio station to meet them forty-eight hours earlier – they might have thought I was proper stalker) and we headed out to see the huge stage. And it was HUGE. As we stood there looking out at an empty Wembley, I got really excited. I wasn't nervous. In fact, I couldn't wait. I got my camera out again and took some more pictures. Then Michelle got her camera out as well. Everybody was really giddy.

Sadly Spinal Tap were not sound-checking for another hour and by now it was time for me to head home and get some rest before the big day.

Saturday 7 July 2007

8.30am

The alarm went off and I woke up feeling knackered. Then I remembered that in a few hours I would be on stage in front of 70,000 people. My feelings of tiredness turned to panic. I needed to get ready, choose my clothes and sort myself out before my pick-up at 11.15. I stuck the kettle on and turned on the TV to see a BBC news report about the concert.

'Are you excited?' asked Sophie.

'Not really,' I said. *'Of course I am I can't wait.'*

I showered, changed, picked my clothes out and double-checked I had everything. Once I was ready, I went into my office, switched the computer on, searched iTunes for Queen and listened to Freddie Mercury singing 'Another One Bites The Dust' live from Wembley in 1986.

'Dee daa dee dar dar daa,' sang Freddie, his voice echoing round the stadium.

'I wanna do that today,' I said to Sophie. 'I wanna stand on stage and sing like Freddie Mercury.'

'More like Freddie Ljungberg with your voice,' replied Sophie.

As I sang along to Queen, the doorbell went. I shouted at Sophie that I had to go, but when I opened the door it wasn't my pick-up but my neighbour Tim.

'Hiya, mate. You all right?' asked Tim.

'Yeah, I'm fine.'

'What time you going to Wembley?' he asked casually.

'Now. I thought you were the guy picking me up.'

'Nah, nah. I've just popped round to see if I can borrow some sunglasses cos it's meant to be sunny today.'

Can you believe this? My next-door neighbour, who incidentally is going to Live Earth today because I got him a ticket, is now asking for sunglasses as I'm about to leave to do one of the biggest gigs of my life!

'Oh, come on in, why don't you. Let's try a few pairs on and see which ones are the best,' I say.

'Cheers, mate, that would be great.' And he walks into my flat. One minute later and he's trying on sunglasses.

'Do these look all right?'

'Yeah, they look fine. Now take them and FUCK OFF!'

11.18am

When I was doing *Live With Chris Moyles* on Channel 5 every week night, I used to get from Radio 1 to the pub/studio on a Virgin taxi bike. Basically it's like a taxi, but it's a motorbike. A guy called Ceri was the boss and he and his drivers would whisk me the few miles through standstill rush-hour traffic to get me to the studio on time. Yesterday I called him and asked if he could help me get to Wembley, as I knew the traffic would be bad. So Russ was sent to get me there on time. Now before you start moaning and saying, 'But, Chris, I thought you were trying to reduce your carbon foot-print and save the environment' – well, yeah, I am, but Rome wasn't built in a day so fuck it. Besides, taxi bikes are very cool. You sit on the back of the motorbike, and that's it. You don't have to do any driving, you just sit there and enjoy the view. As we got nearer the stadium, the traffic started to build up and I started getting all excited again.

When we pulled up, Michelle was waiting for us. One quick cigarette later, and I was back inside Wembley stadium, ready for the day.

12.20pm

I'm in my shared dressing room with Michelle and Fleur (I think she's the boss!). Vernon Kay calls me and we have a live chat about the day. At the end of the conversation, I do something that I've noticed I do more and more these days.

'Big man, have a great day and talk to you soon,' says Vernon.

'Cheers, Vernon. God love.'

God love? What the heck does that mean? Well, it's simple: in my head it was going to be 'God bless', then as soon as I started saying it, I wanted to say 'lots of love'. Hence, 'God love'.

1.15pm

Michelle, Sophie and I head to the stage to get ready for the show. It's great to have Sophie here at things like this. The best thing is that she still gets really excited when she sees me walk out on stage. I run through what I'm going to say and get plugged up with my earpiece. As we stand at the side of the stage, we see the first act walking towards us. It's Roger Taylor, the drummer from Queen, Chad Smith, the drummer from the Red Hot Chili Peppers, and Taylor Hawkins, the drummer from Foo Fighters. Together with what seem to be about forty other drummers, they are to open the show with a massive drum spectacular. Everybody takes their places and the countdown begins. The crowd, which is huge, even though the stadium's not yet full, are surprisingly quiet, until exactly 1.30 when the show begins. The drummers kick off as the three brilliant drummers at the back start banging away. Then they break into the drum intro from Queen's 'We Will Rock You' and the whole crowd, and I mean the entire audience, stick their hands in the air and start clapping. From the side of the stage, looking out from behind our curtain, it looked amazing.

When they finish, the crowd cheer and the opening titles begin.

'Stand by, Chris,' I hear in my ear. 'And good luck.'

I await my introduction.

1.35pm

To prepare the stage for the next band will take about three minutes, and I have roughly prepared what I'm going to say. It doesn't really bother me, because, let's be honest, talking is what I do, and if they needed me to fill for fifteen minutes I'd still need to be told to shut up. They have said that if there is a problem, they will shout the word 'FILL' down my earpiece, and then I will keep going. Other than that, all I have to do is go out, warm the crowd up, then when I hear 'THEY'RE READY', that means the band are ready. I whip the crowd into a frenzy, introduce the band and get the hell off the stage as quick as I can. Simple.

The voice of God booms out across the stadium.

'LADIES AND GENTLEMEN ...'

This is it. Here we go.

'PLEASE WELCOME YOUR HOST ...'

Wow, that does sound weird. I'm the 'host' of a show in front of 70,000 people. It's not like doing Radio Top Shop on Briggate in Leeds, is it?

'HE'S THE SAVIOUR OF BREAKFAST RADIO ...'

At this point, the crowd begin to cheer. Thank God for that, I think to myself. The guy hasn't even said my name yet and I'm getting a good reaction already. This is what I was hoping for, and I really wasn't sure if I'd get it, or how the crowd would react. Imagine getting all the way through the introduction and walking out there to silence. That would be embarrassing.

'THE MAN MOST BRITONS WAKE UP TO ...'

Now I must point out that I didn't write this introduction. Technically Terry Wogan wakes up more Britons than I do. Although you could argue that his audience is so old they probably suffer from arthritis and rheumatism. If that's the case, then half of them can't sleep at night and have probably been awake for hours anyway. So maybe I do actually 'wake up' more Britons than he does. Anyway, I can't chat about this all day, I've got to get on stage.

'HE'S THE FANTASTIC MISTER ...'

Here we go. Don't mess it up, Chris.

'CHRIS MOYLES!'

I walk out from behind the curtain and make my way to the front of the stage. As it's still very early, the stadium's only about half full. So that's only about 35,000 people then. What a doddle! I wait till the crowd dies down and then scream down the microphone:

HELLO, WEMBLEY!

The crowd cheer once more and immediately I feel relaxed and comfortable. Odd, really, when you think about it, but it's easier for me to be on stage talking to thousands of people than to be talking to a few people in a room.

I explain why everybody is here today, to help improve our carbon footprint. I don't have a clue what that means but hey, it's going to be a great concert!

(Obviously that statement is not true. A couple of weeks before today, I had a meeting with the organisers, including a bloody scientist, so that I would understand what the concert was about. However, it's the start of a long day for most of the crowd and all they want right now is to get on with the show.)

I tell the crowd there will be 70,000 people filling Wembley today, and that there are another eight Live Earth concerts taking place around the world. Add to that about 6,000 smaller events and a worldwide television audience – which means that Live Earth will have an estimated audience of about:

2 BILLION PEOPLE

'I never like to miss an opportunity, so with that in mind, would anybody like to buy a car? It's a four-by-four and it's not very good for the environment.'

Amazingly, it gets a laugh. I'm pleased it worked but I think I should really leave it at that and move on.

I run through some of the bands playing and the crowd cheer each time.

RAZORLIGHT

SNOW PATROL

KASABIAN

On stage you can tell if an audience is really up for a gig. However, with events like this, because there are so many bands in the line-up, you're never sure who's going to get a big cheer, and who, if any, will get booed. Now here's a secret about making sure everybody gets a good reaction. If you get to a name you're not sure how the crowd will react to, let's say, for example's sake only, James Blunt, then you stick his name just before somebody you know will get a huge cheer. That way the crowd don't even have time to boo. See, I'm good at this shit!

It works and by the time I get to MADONNA, the crowd are loving it.

As I say her name, I just happen to glance at the stage.

I'd been enjoying myself so much with the crowd that I'd forgotten to listen out for my cue to introduce the band. But then again I haven't actually heard anything in my ear.

I look at the stage and I see the band GENESIS watching me. Phil Collins is sat at the drum kit staring at me.

Jesus, how long have they been there for? I panic a little. Have they been shouting in my ear, telling me that they're ready and I just haven't heard them? Has my earpiece broken? Shit, it doesn't matter, the point is I've been stood talking to the crowd with no idea that this huge group are there in the middle of the stage waiting for me to shut up waffling and introduce them.

'Are you ready? Should we have a go?' I say, and amazingly Phil Collins just gives me a kind of 'Yeah why not' nod. In my ear I hear somebody scream, 'Chris, they're ready now.'

NO SHIT!

I know they're ready cos they're all staring at me!

I tell the crowd that when I point at them I want them to start cheering and not stop. This always builds the noise up and gets a really good reaction for the band. I start pointing to my left and they start cheering. Then I move my hand round the stadium and get everybody else joining in. At this point I'm just saying whatever comes into my head. At one point I hear myself say:

'You're here for a long time and you're here for a good time.'

I can't believe it. I've just gone and used a line from a Huey Lewis and the News record from years ago. Still, it doesn't matter because nobody will notice.

Sitting at home watching on television is my friend Comedy Dave. He texts me immediately.

'First ever use of a Huey Lewis line at the new Wembley, mate. Well done.'

Smart arse.

I introduce Genesis and run off the stage as quick as I can.

As Genesis play, I stand behind a curtain at the side of the stage again. It was a great place to be because every single act on the stage had to walk past and we got to see everybody. I notice Eddie Izzard pacing up and down looking all serious as if he's trying to memorise what he's going to say on stage. He sees me and I say hello and introduce myself. This is often a bad idea. Even though he's been on the radio show before for an interview, I can't be sure he'll remember who I am, let alone like me. I know I'm paranoid, but it's the truth. But I'm on a high so I give it a go anyway.

'Nice to see you again. I'm Chris Moyles,' I say.

I'm never sure how that statement will be received. Sometimes you might get back: 'Hey, Chris, I remember you, how are you?' And sometimes you might not.

As it turns out, he seems at least to know who I am, and we chat about what the crowd's like. So that went well.

However, later that day my paranoia went into overdrive.

I was running around backstage when I bumped into a woman called Barbara Charone. This lady is one of the most powerful people in the publicity business, with a client list that includes Madonna. Barbara also loves our radio show and has a loud voice.

'Oh my God, I love you,' she shouts in her American accent. 'Your radio show is so funny. I was listening yesterday and you were really making me laugh.' As we walk down the corridor, with Barbara hanging off me like a lovable fan, we walk straight into Guy Ritchie, husband to Madonna.

'Hey, Guy, do you know this man?' asks Barbara.

Guy Ritchie's face makes no expression whatsoever as he replies:

'No.'

Oh Jesus, this will be fun.

'Hi, Guy, I'm Chris, nice to meet you.' I put out my hand to shake his.

Again, his face doesn't move. You'd think I'd just pissed down his trousers.

'Oh my God, I love this guy, I listen to the Chris Moyles show every day,' shrieks Barbara.

'Oh right, Chris Moyles,' says Guy, looking about 3 per cent more interested than he did a few seconds earlier. Now I have to work out if I've ever slagged him off on the radio, or whether he's just a miserable bloke. Either way I don't want to stay to find out, so I make my excuses and leave.

The rest of the day at Wembley was pretty much the same. I met *Doctor Who*'s David Tennant washing his hands in the boys' toilet. (Well, he'd hardly use the girls', would he?) Dave Grohl from Foo Fighters introduced me to his family. Actor Kyle MacLachlan told me that I had done a good job hosting the show. Chris Rock asked if I was a comedian and we had our photo taken together. And Graham Norton told me that he'd only had three glasses of wine all day. It was an interesting few hours to say the least.

And then right at the end of the day, when I didn't think it could get any better, Michelle who had been looking after me all day, presented me with the sign saying 'CHRIS MOYLES' that she'd nicked off the dressing-room door. God bless her.

PATRICK KIELTY ON MOYLES

People underestimate Chris. He is not just the saviour of Radio 1 but, in my opinion, is the saviour of radio in this country full stop. In a world of multi-choice entertainment, his massive popularity with listeners is a testimony to his unequalled originality, unending creativity, razor-sharp wit and a truly unique built-in radar for what the nation really wants to hear.

Which is just as well cos he's shit on the telly.

Q&A
Genuine Questions from My Radio Audience

So one morning on the radio I asked my listeners if they wanted to ask me anything. The following are REAL questions from real people.

DAVID EVANS FROM COLWYN BAY

Q: Are you a madras or a vindaloo man?

A: Actually I am a very simple 'chicken curry with no onions' man.

PAUL FROM STOURBRIDGE

Q: As an adult, have you ever wet the bed after a night drinking?

A: I am delighted to inform you, Paul, that I have NEVER wet the bed as an adult. However, occasionally I do go what I call 'Dead Man Walking'. This is when I get up in the middle of the night and try and find the bathroom in the dark, resulting in me walking around the bedroom with my arms stretched out in front of me like some kind of monster. Now I know many people have done, or even still do this, but I promise you that my Dead Man Walking has never resulted in me pissing in the wardrobe or taking a dump on top of the chest of drawers. Once in Dublin, though, after a lot of beers, I got up in the middle of the night to go to the bathroom. After twenty minutes I still wasn't back in bed. Sophie walked into the bathroom only to catch me stood in the shower completely naked, with the shower switched off.

'What are you doing?' she asked me.

'I'm having a shower, of course,' was my reply.

Drink is an evil friend sometimes!

MARK MEARS

Q: At what point in your life did you decide you were going to be a radio presenter?

A: Buy my first book, Mark, you cheap git!

LAUREN KAY

Q: Chris, do you think you would like yourself if you met you?

A: I'd like to think so. I would probably really like me sometimes, but also think I was a bit of an arse other times. But I don't think I'd like to be me. How does that grab you for some psychological bullshit?

GARETH YARDLEY FROM HULL

Q: Have you ever got into a fight with another fan at a Leeds United game, and if so, who?

A: You sound like a nice, relaxed young man, Gareth, with no issues at all! The only time I ever got near to a fight at a Leeds game was when the woman behind the bar charged me £6 for two glasses of

Coke. With those bar prices I don't know how they ever got into debt!

MIKE LI FROM LUTON

Q: I honestly believe that you and your team saved my life. Is there anyone who you believe saved your life?

A: Whoever makes Carling lager.

PETER THOMAS FROM MABLETHORPE

Q: Do you ever read these questions?

A: Yes.

STACY McQUEEN FROM NEWBURY

Q: You are having a dinner party and you can invite five people, living or dead. Who would they be, and why?

A: Well, first of all they would have to be alive. I couldn't bear an evening with a load of dead dudes. If you want to spend the night with a room full of people who look like death, turn up at the next Radio 1 DJ dinner!

RICHARD FROM LEICESTER

Q: Do you consider yourself lucky to have been born in an age where there is a genuine lack of talent on Radio 1?

A: Cheeky sod.

ANONYMOUS

Q: Chris, can you ride a bicycle?

A: Sure. Where and when?

FIONA FORSYTH FROM BIRMINGHAM

Q: How much money did you make from your first book?

A: Well, my publishers promised me that they only made £100 but it cost £99 to print.

DAN SHAKIR FROM LONDON

Q: What's the greatest Leeds goal you've ever seen?

A: I've seen MANY great goals at Elland Road, but sadly they were all AGAINST Leeds. However, I was at Crystal Palace when Harry Kewell scored a brilliant goal, running all the way from the halfway line straight towards Berthelin. He fired the ball into the back of the net, fell over and sat on his arse pulling his socks up as the rest of the Leeds fans went mental. Perhaps not the best ever, but one that sticks in my mind.

HOLLY CLARKE FROM STOCKPORT

Q: What's the worst thing you got into trouble for at school?

A: Probably arson.

HUGH KENNEDY FROM WEST MIDLANDS

Q: Have you ever pulled one of your guests?

A: I don't think it would be gentleman-like to reveal something so personal. All I'll say is, ask Will Young. The naughty boy.

JAMES T FROM SURREY

Q: Would you ever consider getting the same bus as Aled?

A: I don't get buses, James. I'm a taxi man. Besides, I don't think his bus goes my way!

CRAIG DALTON FROM PERTH

Q: If you could have been in any film ever, what film, and which character would you have played?

A: I think it would have been cool to have played Han Solo in *Star Wars*, or equally Marty McFly in *Back To The Future*. Or the fella from *Confessions of a Window Cleaner*. That might have been fun.

DAWN FROM THE ISLE OF SHEPPEY

Q: You always put fat people down, so how do you live with yourself?

A: Good question, Dawn. The simple answer is I couldn't live with myself, so I had to move next door. But that meant that my neighbours were fat also, so I moved back.

STEVEN SHUTTLEWORTH FROM KEIGHLEY

Q: If you weren't a DJ, what other job would you want to do?

A: Easy. I would love to be Bono, or Liam Gallagher, or Robbie Williams, or Freddie Mercury. I have always wanted to be a rock star. Or an actor. Then again I probably would've ended up sitting on a park bench drinking all day.

SHIRLEY FROM INVERNESS

Q: How important do you think you are in the entertainment business on a scale of 1 to 10?

A: Well, I suppose I would say a 5. That's a safe answer I reckon. I mean I'm not as important as John Lennon, but hopefully higher on the list than Timmy Mallet!

MIKE JOY FROM BROADSTAIRS

Q: What are your thoughts on male thongs?

A: Whatever floats your boat, Mike.

DANNI DADSWELL FROM STOKE-ON-TRENT

Q: In your first book you said you worked at Radio Top Shop. Would you ever go back and do the breakfast show from the shop floor? If so, you could create your own version of supermarket sweep but with clothes!

A: Jesus Christ, what are you on? Why the hell would I want to do that?

NICHOLA SCHOLES FROM LEIGH

Q: Dry roasted or salted nuts?

A: Salted every time, Nichola.

RACHEL COLLINSON

Q: Thanks, Chris – you've helped me laugh in the morning when it's been hard for me as I've been ill. My question is who were your comedy influences?

A: Well, Rachel, before I answer your question, may I say it was a pleasure making you laugh in the morning when you weren't well. And also thank you so much for asking me that question and therefore letting me put it in the book, making me look as if I make a difference in people's lives and turning me into something other than a big-headed DJ. That said, in answer to your question, in no particular order:

Vic and Bob
Cannon and Ball
Benny Hill

The Two Ronnies

Chubby Brown

Eddie Izzard

Howard Stern

Steve Wright

Nick Abbot

My dad

Uncle Jim

Uncle Tom

And everybody else that I have stolen material from!

LILY LEVIN FROM SOUTHAM

Q: What would you do if you were the only person left in the world? Nothing is different except there are no people.

A: I LOVE this question. It's like the beginning of the movie *28 Days Later*. Imagine London, completely empty, except me. Wicked. So again in no particular order:

Ride around on a shopping trolley through Piccadilly Circus.

Drive up the M1 in the fastest car I could find.

Replace the turf at Wembley with loads of sofas from nearby empty houses, making it look like the biggest living room in the world.

Go to Top Shop and dress up as Cher.

Drive an underground train.

Go to my local pub and get my free barrel of beer that I'm owed!

VICKY ALLEN FROM PLYMOUTH

Q: If you were a superhero, who would you be and why?

A: Donut-man. Nuff said.

LEA RIDLEY FROM NUNEATON

Q: Have you ever had a dream where a giant pillow is chasing you and you are struggling to run away?

A: Erm, no.

DONNA BEARMAN, AN AUSSIE FROM BRIGHOUSE

Q: How much of your show is impromptu and how much is scripted?

A: We often joke about this question on the radio, normally right after we have just ended up in a very strange off-the-cuff conversation. The answer is that most of the show is ad-libbed. Hardly anything is scripted, unless it's a competition read or something like that. If you've ever listened to more than one whole show, you'd know that we would NEVER write a script like that!

ALEX HEAP IN WALES

Q: Have you ever eaten a peanut butter sandwich while stroking a llama with your shoes untied?

A: Of course, who hasn't?

DARREN TAYLOR ON THE A14

Q: Will you move to Radio 2 in the future if they offer you a job?

A: I honestly don't believe they ever would. Really. I mean this is what I do now, the show isn't going to change that much and I just don't believe Radio 2 would think I'd fit in. And also, I genuinely love Radio 1 so I can't imagine ever leaving. Besides, I have photos of our boss which he wants to keep quiet so that pretty much keeps me in work!

KELLY SPAIN IN CHESTER

Q: Just wondering, Chris – have you ever danced in front of the mirror naked, saying 'I love my man boobs'?

A: I think that question says more about you than it does me, Kelly!

PETE DOWNES FROM BROMSGROVE

Q: Did you have the opportunity to be a judge on the TV show *The X Factor* and, if so, why did you turn it down?

A: Simple answer, I was NEVER offered the job. When Louis Walsh was fired, the newspapers ran a story saying that he was out and I was in. I was never contacted by Simon Cowell or anybody on the show. The papers continued to run the story and after a week even I thought I had the job. A few months later, Louis and Simon have patched things up and Louis is back on the show. Shame, because I would have liked to be a judge. Can you imagine me sitting between Sharon Osbourne and Simon Cowell?

'I think she's fit, let's put her through.'

'But Chris, she can't sing a note.'

'Who cares? Look at her. Well done, my darling, you're through to the next stage. Right, who's next?'

JESS JAMES FROM GLOUCESTER

Q: Who are your top five celebs that, even though you're in a relationship, you're allowed!?

A: Ha. Sophie and I have joked about this before. It's called 'The Allowed List'. Sophie has an odd list of famous people that she once fancied, or still does, including Liam Gallagher, Jay Kay from Jamiroquai and Thierry Henry. My list is more simplistic than that. Basically it's anybody who'd say 'Yes', apart from Lisa Riley and Louis Walsh!

ROB HAMPSON IN MANCHESTER

Q: As there is a delay on the time pips on digital radio, does the move away from analogue mean we will travel back in time?

A: Erm, no.

TRISH FROM SHEFFIELD

Q: When are you going to take your head from up your bum?

A: Wednesday, about tea time-ish.

STEVE THOMAS FROM CHELTENHAM

Q: Chris, do you worry about the show's popularity coming to an end?

A: Now this is a tough one to answer. Of course, I know that we won't always have the most high-profile show on the radio, although I would like to have the best show for as long as I can. In the world of Radio 1 each show naturally has a shelf life – some last longer than others so who knows if and when our time will run out? I'd like to work for Radio 1 for as long as I can, as I genuinely love the station. However, if that day does come it's my dream to be able to pick the show up and simply take it to another radio station. If the audience like what we're doing now, then hopefully they always will. I suppose that's quite an idealistic answer, but it's the truth. Nobody seems to get bored with Terry Wogan. His audience love him and will stay with him until he decides he's had enough. That's exactly what I'd like to do. So in a weird way, Wogan is my role model!

RACHAEL CAPENER FROM SWINDON

Q: I have been known to walk, talk and even smoke in my sleep. What have you done in your sleep?

A: Jesus, why are so many people interested in what I do when I'm drunk? There was a time years ago when I was back at home staying at my parents' house in Leeds. I'd been out with some friends and had a few drinks. In the middle of the night, my mum heard me get up and go downstairs. She listened out for a while and when I didn't come back upstairs, she got out of her bed and went to look for me. She opened the lounge door to find me sitting crossed legged in the dark, completely stark naked. When she asked me what I was doing, I told her I was playing on my Playstation. I didn't have a Playstation!

MICHAEL OLLIFFE FROM KENT

Q: What was it like driving to the Brit Awards with Jeremy Clarkson in the amazing stretch limo?

A: I have been really lucky with my job to have done some very cool stuff, and this was definitely one of those times.

I was asked if I'd take part in a film for *Top Gear* where Jeremy would indeed drive me to the Brits in a specially designed and custom-built stretch limousine. Being a fan of the show I knew that it wouldn't be your average limo but I didn't care. I just thought it was cool to be asked. They sent a car to pick me up and take me over to Chelsea Harbour where they were ready to film. Incidentally I don't live anywhere near this place, and when we started filming, I had to pretend to be leaving my flat. A flat I didn't actually live in. TV is all a lie, you know. Jeremy met me and walked me to the car. It was a stretch Panda limo. A 1993 one-litre Fiat Panda CLX, to be precise.

I climbed in, and used the trolley and rope system to reach the seat at the back of the car. If you've ever seen the film *The Great Escape*, then imagine that, but instead of a tunnel full of soil and gravel, it was a stretch Panda.

Originally Jeremy had made the car to be forty-six feet long. However, it didn't pass the inspection to be road legal, so he chopped seven feet out of the middle. So now, as Jeremy proudly told me, it was only 'eight feet longer than a bus'.

We then made our way through the streets of London towards Earls Court where the Brits were taking place. If you've seen the TV footage of our journey it's very funny indeed, but let me also tell you that it was all FOR REAL. I sat in the back of a thirty-eight-foot-long stretch Panda car for over two hours as we made our way through traffic and down streets that were barely wide enough for the car to move.

Then, just as we were on the final straight, the car split into two. There on the street, it just seemed to 'snap' in the middle. I climbed out of the back, and Jeremy and I pulled both sections of the car apart. Undefeated, we got in the front seats, and pulled away, leaving half a Panda, albeit nineteen feet of it, lying by the side of the road.

We did, though, eventually arrive. The back of the broken car was scraping the road as sparks flew everywhere, and the trolley pulley system was dragging behind us. It's fair to say that we made one hell of an entrance.

It was one of the funniest things that I've done and it was such a laugh, despite being embarrassing as well. I met Richard Hammond at an awards event a few months later and he told me that it was one of the funniest things he had ever seen on *Top Gear*. Jeremy Clarkson and myself, huddled in the front seats of a stretch Panda limo that had split into two pieces, with Jeremy saying:

'Wait, let me get the door for you. *Dignity* ...'

'Oh yeah. *Dignity!*'

RYAN FROM CORNWALL

Q: How did you manage to pull Sophie, you fat git?

A: I don't know, Ryan. I suppose I was just lucky that you weren't around at the time, you charmer!

ANDI FROM LONDON

Q: Do you have the same conversations down the pub that you have on the show but with added swearing? Given the choice, would you like the option to swear on the radio show, like Gordon the Chef?

A: Like Gordon the Chef? You say that as if your mate is a chef called Gordon. I take it you mean Gordon Ramsay. Well, he is indeed a foul-mouthed little fucker and you wouldn't hear such language from myself. In all honesty though, it would be nice to have more freedom on the show. It would be great to be able to tell a story the same way that you would tell it down the pub. I wouldn't necessarily want to swear as such, but it would certainly make the show feel more natural, I think. If a story could be enhanced by the odd swear word then that would be great but I wouldn't just swear for the sake of it. That would sound very strange.

'OK, enough of this bullshit, here's Dominic with the mother fucking travel news.'

I just don't think so.

DARREN IN MANCHESTER

Q: Have you ever dreamed about doing it with one of the people working on your show, and was it Dave?

A: Erm, NO.

JOHN SEWELL FROM LEEDS

Q: Have you ever used the line 'Do you know who I am?' and, if
so, where and when?

A: I have NEVER used that line because it would be so embarrassing.
Imagine using it, only to get the reply, 'No I have no idea who you
are. Who are you?'

   The only time I ever came close to saying something along those
lines, is when I'm trying to get into the Radio 1 building, and that's
the truth. Occasionally I will leave my BBC ID at home, and then
try to convince the security guard that I am doing the show
starting at 7 o'clock.

   *'See those DJ photos over there? Well, see the one that looks like
me?'*

STEVE KIRK FROM BOLTON

Q: Chris, have you ever fallen asleep on the toilet?

A: Honestly, yes, loads of times. I must point out, though, that this is
always early in the morning when I am half asleep. I don't
normally drop off whilst mid-flow, if you get my drift. But it has
been known sometimes for me to sit on the toilet lid and just doze
off. The worst thing is waking up and trying to work out how long
I've been sat there.

TINA PRICE FROM LAMPETER, WALES

Q: Have you ever wanted to tell your producers where to stick
it halfway through the show?

A: Well, as you may know if you listen regularly to the show, I keep those
emotions very quiet! All right, I have been known on occasion to blurt
out what's in my head when it comes to both Rachel and Aled, and
occasionally I might just tell them to get out of the studio where I

can't see them – but normally I calm down fairly quickly. I also get annoyed at myself during the show so it's not just Rachel and Aled that have to suffer. Plus I'm not the only one that gets moody sometimes. Honestly, you should see Aled's face when we don't get time to play a Justin Timberlake record. Now that's scary.

LUKE BATTEN FROM ADDLESTONE

Q: Who do you think would win in a fight between Batman and Spiderman?

A: Nice question, Luke, and sadly I have to say Batman, I think. I prefer Spiderman, but I do think that he would get his ass kicked. The simple reason is that Batman is a man, whereas Spiderman is only a boy. I myself recently invented a superhero called Donutman. He eats donuts. I think I would like to play him in a movie sometime, so if there are any Hollywood movie directors reading this, feel free to get in touch.

LYNDSEY CRAWFORD FROM THE WIRRAL

Q: If you could be someone else for the day, who would you be?

A: Peter Andre.

PAUL NORRIE IN POOLE

Q: What is the best freebie that you've been given?

A: A lot of stuff is sent in to the show in the hope that we mention it on the air. Sometimes though, people send stuff just for us and it's always nice to get a free pair of trainers or some cool T-shirts. I still get really excited about being given free CDs. Even though it's been happening for years and it's a requirement in this job, I love getting albums sent to me before they are released. An added bonus with this is that when a band plays a gig on the night their new album is released, you can watch them and sing along while nobody else knows the words!

ANDREW WRIGHT FROM RHYL

Q: What is your favourite takeaway food?

A: You can ask me anything and this is what you choose? It would have to be a toss-up between Chinese, Indian, pizza, burgers, Italian and fish and chips. Not all together though.

ANONYMOUS

Q: Does Sophie have any pet names for you?

A: Donkey, Three-legs, and Gorgeous Man. I think 'Shut Up' is one cos I seem to hear that enough too.

HELEN STUBBS IN SUNDERLAND

Q: A freak accident happens and the future of the human race depends on you and your radio show team. Who would it be, Rachel or Carrie?

A: To what, help save the human race? In that case, we're all screwed.

PHIL B FROM ESSEX

Q: Do you have any hobbies? If so, what are they?

A: Well, for the past few years I have been collecting white lines. Already I have a vast collection that I keep on various different roads throughout the UK.

LOUISE WILLIAMS FROM NORTHAMPTON

Q: If you had the chance to do everything all over again, would you live your life the same or would you choose a different path?

A: I wouldn't do anything differently, except believe people when they told me that eating certain foods would make me fat.

COLIN KNAPP FROM CHELMSFORD

Q: Do you get annoyed with all these TV personalities getting into radio through an easy route, when you spent years learning your trade and building your name?

A: I kind of did at first, yeah. I'm proud to work at Radio 1 and see it as quite an achievement to have got a job there. So when certain people just waltzed into the station and got a show offered to them on a plate, it used to piss me off. Then again, I think Vernon Kay is brilliant on the radio and I think Fearne Cotton is great as well so what can you do. Besides, a lot of people can't cut it on radio and it's always nice to see them fail. (You know who you are if you're reading this!)

PHIL CLARK FROM STAFFORD

Q: Did you ever do DJ sets at local clubs when you worked in the Stoke area?

A: Actually for a short while I did Saturday nights upstairs at The Reynolds Club in Stafford. Well, I did until I got fired from the local radio station, then when I turned up to gig at the nightclub, they thought that because I'd been fired I wouldn't turn up, so they booked somebody else.

'Oh, that's OK. Just give me my money and I'll go home?'

'Money for what?' I remember they asked.

'Well, I'm booked for tonight, and I've turned up. You've booked somebody else and didn't bother telling me. So pay me, and I'll go home. No hard feelings,' I said with a big smile.

It didn't work, though. In fact not only did I not get paid, but on the way home I got stopped for speeding and later in court I got three points, a two-week ban and a fine. I have never been back to Stafford.

MATT GIORDMANIA FROM BASILDON, ESSEX

Q: If you were stuck in a broken lift with Drew Barrymore and Halle Berry for eight hours, what would you say to them and why? I'd just be moody and stroppy with them and see what they would do? Ha!

A: You evil man, Matt. I, however, would charm the pair of these ladies into thinking that I was actually a very misunderstood hunk. I'd amaze them with my impressions of famous people and do cute faces. Once they were convinced, I would work my Jedi mind trick on them and get them both to ask me out for dinner – then turn down Halle Berry and say Yes to Drew. Later, after we'd been released, I would say Yes to Halle's offer, and explain that I hadn't wanted to hurt Drew's feelings by turning her down, knowing that Halle could handle the rejection, as she was older and wiser. I may have thought about this question too much.

RHIAN THOMAS FROM SWANSEA

Q: Is this a clever plan to get all the people who ask questions to buy your book to see if their questions are in it so you get more sales?

A: Yes.

LEE PEDZISZ

Q: Whilst pouring hot water on to an ants' nest to kill them, have you ever shouted, 'I AM YOUR KING, I AM TOP OF THE FOOD CHAIN. HA HA!'?

A: No.

RAY IRVINE FROM COVENTRY

Q: If you could be Inspector Gadget for a day, which part of your body would you 'Go Go Gadget Go' and why?

A: Jesus, I'm getting tired now.

SETH EVANS FROM BARNSLEY

Q: Do you ever wish you came from Barnsley and not Leeds?

A: Nope. I love Leeds. I love Yorkshire, and generally anywhere in the North. Then it's England, then the UK and finally Europe. And in that order too.

SOPHIE WAITE, AT HOME

Q: Have you finished writing yet?

A: Yes, honey.